P9-DCP-701

KISS MY TIARA

KISS MY TIARA

HOW TO RULE THE WORLD AS A SMARTMOUTH GODDESS

SUSAN JANE GILMAN

WARNER BOOKS

NEW YORK   BOSTON

If you purchase this book without a cover you should be aware that this book may have been stolen property and reported as "unsold and destroyed" to the publisher. In such case neither the author nor the publisher has received any payment for this "stripped book."

Copyright © 2001 by Susan Jane Gilman
All rights reserved.

Sections in Chapters 1, 2, 10, and 23 originally appeared in a different form in *HUES* magazine, Vol. IV, issues 2–5, and Vol. V, issue 1, and are reprinted with acknowledgment and gratitude to New Moon Publishing.

Sections from Chapter 4 originally appeared in abbreviated form in the *Los Angeles Times* copyright 1998 and are reprinted by permission of the Los Angeles Times.

Sections in Chapter 23 were originally published in the *New York Times*, Sept. 1, 1991, copyright 1991 and are reprinted by permission of the New York Times Co.

The quote on page 129 appears by permission of Madonna and Miramax Film Corp.

Lyrics from "Chopsticks" copyright 1995 Liz Phair & Matador Records and "Shitloads of Money" copyright 1998 Liz Phair & Capitol Records are both reprinted by permission of Liz Phair.

Warner Books

Time Warner Book Group
1271 Avenue of the Americas, New York, NY 10020
Visit our Web site at www.twbookmark.com

Printed in the United States of America

First Printing: February 2001
10

Library of Congress Cataloging-in-Publication Data
Gilman, Susan Jane.
    Kiss my tiara: how to rule the world as a smartmouth goddess/
by Susan Jane Gilman.
        p.   cm.
    ISBN 0-446-67577-6
    1. Women—Conduct of life. Title.
BJ1610.G55 2001
305.4'02'07—dc21

00-032486

Cover design by Raquel Jaramillo
Book design by Nancy Singer Olaguera
Text composition by Peng Olaguera

*This book is dedicated to
the memory of my grandmother*

Elizabeth Gilman

who insisted on living life her own way.

Contents

ගා

Introduction
ꔸ

Forget Rules for Catching a Husband. How 'bout Rules for Catching a Life?

My grandma never said, "Let him take the lead."
My grandma said, "Have another piece of cake and wash it down with a gin and tonic."

For centuries, lovers, philosophers, and marketers alike have pondered the question, "What do women want?" Having been an editor for a young women's magazine—and being a woman myself—I've come to find that most women today want two things: (1) some smart, no-nonsense advice about how to navigate the world, and (2) to laugh. Ideally, we want both these things at once.

Face it, today's world is full of contradictory messages and expectations for young women. Why else would platform sneakers have been such a hit with us? We post–Baby Boom Babes suffer from conflicting impulses. "If only I could balance my life the way I balance my checkbook," a friend of mine recently moaned. ("If only I could *find* my checkbook," said another.)

Women of my generation have acquired all the responsibilities that come with sexual equality (i.e., earn your own paycheck), but few of the equal benefits (again: see *paycheck*). We're encouraged to be "empowered" but vilified for being feminists. We have more career opportunities than ever, but somehow we still get the message that a bustier, not a brain, is the real source of "Girl Power." We're urged to put on Nike cross-trainers and "Just Do It"—but we're encouraged to "just do it" while consuming twelve hundred calories a day and weighing no more than 103 pounds. We're inspired to scale the corporate ladder, but we're fully aware that it still bumps up against the glass ceiling—and that, more often than not, some guy is still peeking up our skirts as we climb.

Of course, pressure to get married and have kids is always buzzing in our ears like societal Muzak: *Hurry up! Your clock is ticking!* Unless, of course, we're gay—in which case we experience pressure to "straighten up." And all the while we know that we probably have it better than any group of women in history. But we're still fraught with ambivalence over choices.

Throughout all of this, sadly, many women's personal battles are not in the boardrooms or courtrooms but in our own bathrooms. Though the women's movement has done a lot over the past few decades to right the scales of justice, it has had little effect on our own scales and mirrors. For so many women, our physical appearance is a major hurdle to feeling powerful and confident. And we just can't seem to get over this. "Want to know what today's chic young feminist thinkers care about?" *Time* magazine crowed recently. "Their bodies! Themselves!" Much as I hate to side with *Time*, it's true that some of us literally can't see past the nose on our face.

And while we're sitting there immobilized before the mirror, we're reading backlashy, boy-crazy women's magazines that instruct us to do stuff like master the "art" of fellatio, wrap our thighs in cellophane, or "put your panties in the freezer, then mail them to *him* at his office in an envelope full of confetti!"

On top of these, of course, we've also read *The Rules*.

The Rules came out, like, what, a zillion years ago? And yet people still refer to them so often, you'd think they were the Ten Commandments.

The Rules essentially instructed women to act like diet soda. Be effervescent! Sweet! Chronically artificial! Remain bubbly and fluid, they implied, and you could trick a guy into marrying you.

For us progressive prima donnas, *The Rules*, at first glance, was nothing but a warmed-over version of the "trade your hymen for a diamond" formula that nice girls followed in the fifties. But the book was seductive. Why? Precisely because it offered, well, *rules*. It gave young women very clear instructions: *Follow these*, it promised, *and you will live happily ever after*. It was a guaranteed formula—a godsend! Finally, tangible guidelines! Order amidst the chaos!

And the clincher? These "time-tested secrets" supposedly came from Grandma. Who could be more comforting and wise than Grandma? Who can resist Grandma?

In today's day and age, oh, how we want Grandma! How we crave reassurance and permission and advice! How we long for a wise, maternal female to help us navigate an increasingly complicated world—a world where all the old bets are off, the new ones are risky, and the payoffs are less certain. Some women long for Grandma so badly, we buy books called *Chicken Soup for the Soul*, co-authored by two guys.

The problem, however, is that some of us don't want a grandma who's fixated on getting us married off. "Catching a husband" sounds a little too much to us like catching a cold. We'd rather act up than settle down. Sure, we want love, but we're also a little ambitious. We have passions and interests and dreams.

Too often, women are confronted with the social equivalent of Sophie's choice. Which "children" are we willing to sacrifice, we're asked: our hearts or our minds? our independence or the prospect of intimacy? our careers or our families? Although we're aware that "having it all" may not be realistic (or even desirable), we don't want to relinquish one part of our soul for another. We want to achieve some balance and richness in our lives. We still want to prevail.

We'd like a sage female voice to counteract all those other grandmas telling us to lose weight, grab that engagement ring, and produce grandchildren before our clock runs out. We'd like a voice to help us deflect all the negative and contradictory messages that fill our heads every day. We'd like a guardian angel perched on our shoulders, helping us to stand tall, be ourselves, and not take any shit. Never mind "self-esteem" and "self-help." We want a bad attitude, thank you, and a good set of power tools.

Well, that's why I've written *Kiss My Tiara*.

For in certain ways traditional feminism just isn't cutting it with us. For women today, feminism is often perceived as dreary. As elitist, academic, Victorian, whiny, and passé. And to some extent—Goddess forgive me for saying this—it's true. I'm not knocking the women's movement of the past years. I'm a huge advocate and beneficiary of choice, workplace-protection laws, and domestic-violence legislation. But I also realize that feminism seventies-style is just about the only trend from the disco era that young women today have not rushed to resurrect. Rhetoric about "reconfiguring the phallocentric modalities of the patriarchy," just turns us into zombies. A lot of us could do without the folk singers, too, thank you, not to mention the Birkenstocks and the sanctimonious veganism. I mean, some of us prefer slaughtering sacred cows to eating tofu any day.

But really, the problem is that a lot of feminist ideology simply doesn't translate well into real life. *It doesn't empower young women on a practical level.* Even media-savvy Naomi Wolf offers prescriptives like, "Let us start with a reinterpretation of 'beauty' that is *noncompetitive, nonhierarchical,* and *nonviolent.*" Sounds good, but does anyone actually know how to do this? For that matter, does anyone have the time? Hell, I barely have time to do my laundry, let alone overhaul the aesthetics of Western civilization.

We Short-Attention-Span Gals could use some practical magic, if you will. Some *unconventional, empowering common sense.* Some smart, neofeminist rules. And it's important that these rules address the whole range of concerns in our lives that we're struggling to balance—love, money, health, food, careers—not just politics, not just husband-catching, not just orgasms. For us, these issues are all tangled together.

And instead of casting us as victims, we'd like a manifesto—excuse me, a womanifesto—that draws upon our strengths.

Well, that's where my grandma—and this book—come in. My grandma never said things like, "Let him take the lead." My grandma was a midget Amazon. A combination of Fran Lebowitz, Queen Latifah, and Jesse Ventura. My grandma campaigned for women's rights, welfare rights, workers' rights—but cut in front of her in the bank line and she'd kill you. She was the type of woman you'd want standing behind you when you're negotiating a raise *or* getting ready for a hot date. My grandma said things like, "Have another piece of cake and wash it down with a gin and tonic." My grandma said things like, "Take a few lovers, travel the world, and don't take any crap."

And she's hardly the first grandma like this in the universe. For the thousands of grandmothers who tells girls to keep their legs crossed and not to wear white shoes after Labor Day, there are always a few salty matriarchs who encourage us to put on a pair of psychological Doc Martens and venture out fearlessly in search of love, glory, and adventure.

This "rules" book is infused with their spirit. It's a voice of irreverent reason to help young women triumph—to help us resist the toxic values of our culture—through chutzpah, intelligence, humor, and feasible action. It is, in short, a guide to wit, power, and attitude.

Because, as I said before: The second thing most women want is to laugh. We gals know instinctively that humor is the most effective weapon—and power tool—we can have in our arsenal. After all, it fulfills a double purpose: It's forceful without being threatening, and it allows us to be subversive with a smile. What better way to bridge our conflicting desires? What better way to reconcile a contradictory world?

Besides, there is so much comedy in gender relations, it's not funny. For example: Just a few years ago, a breast-cancer study was conducted on *men*. Or, in another move that Monty Python could've scripted, legislators actually tried to get health-insurance companies to cover Viagra but not birth control or fertility treatments. Or, take the fact that a bunch of Christian extremists actually got men to spend their whole weekend huddling in a football stadium—away from their wives and children—to demonstrate their devotion to family values. I mean, you can't make this stuff up.

We gals know an absurd world when we see it.

To address women's issues *without* humor in this day and age is sort of criminally negligent. Because, really, it's the only sane choice. If we don't use humor and irreverence, what are the alternatives? Anger, fear, and victimhood—and Goddess knows we've had enough of *that*.

Also, since we gals generally prefer reading menus to following instruction booklets, the chapters in *Kiss My Tiara* can be read à la carte, either *sequentially* or *individually*. In this way, it's a profoundly pro-choice book, sort of like the Yellow Pages. Just open it up and read about whatever grabs you at the moment.

Last, even though this book is meant to be funny—and thus neatly sidesteps any pretenses of speaking the Definitive Truth for All Women—a few confessions are in order.

We progressive prima donnas are often sticklers for inclusion and diversity. Yet, in putting this together, I drew upon the insights of a very limited pool of women. Yeah, they were from different races, religions, and ethnicities. Yeah, some were gay, some were bisexual, and some were straight. And, yeah, while the majority of them were middle class, there were a few waitresses and debutantes thrown in.

But mostly the women had one overriding characteristic: They each had a big, fresh mouth and a laugh that could peel paint off a wall. And if that makes this book in any way homogenous and elitist, so be it. As my grandma used to say, "Fuck 'em if they can't take a joke!"

Part I

ɕʘ

Mistress of Our Domain

Chapter 1

ꙮ

Beauty Tips from
Mental Institutions

---

*"Any girl can be glamourous.
All you have to do is stand still
and look stupid."*
—HEDY LAMARR

A while ago, I got a call from my brother. "Guess what I'm doing?" he said. "I'm making Cindy Crawford's tits bigger."

As a production assistant for *Esquire*, it was his job to digitally "improve" centerfold shots taken by the magazine's photographers. If the editor-in-chief decided that Naomi Campbell's waist should be smaller or Christy Turlington's eyes darker, my brother would have to perform virtual plastic surgery on them: tucking a tummy, bolstering a breast, or bluing an eye with a click of the mouse. "Sometimes we change the women's photographs so much, they look nothing like the original," he said. "I mean, they might as well be Marge Simpson."

Marge Simpson?

Uh-oh.

It used to be, if we gals wanted to look like a model, all we had to do was be born with extraordinary genes, grow to five-foot ten, subsist on lettuce, and maybe develop a coke habit. Now, it seems, we've also got to have our looks "enhanced" by an underpaid production assistant with a fifty-thousand-gigabyte hard drive.

As my grandmother used to say: *Oy*.

Now, I'm not dissing beauty. I love to feel like *all that*; I'm a fetishist for Viva Glam lipstick as much as the next gal. But, frankly, so much of what passes for the business of beauty these days seems to have been concocted by the inmates of a mental institution.

Pluck out all your eyebrows so you can draw them back on with a pencil.

Pay a doctor to remove the fat from your ass and inject it into your chin.

To make your legs look fabulous, wear shoes that will give you varicose veins and bunions.

Have leaky water balloons surgically embedded in your chest.

I mean, if I didn't know better, I'd think these ideas were the ramblings of Quack-Quack, the paranoid schizophrenic dressed in Saran Wrap and duct tape who used to hang around my corner and shout at the local women, "I shoot poison in your face! I cut off your chin!"

Too bad Quack-Quack couldn't get his act together and become a plastic surgeon on Madison Avenue, because these are exactly the things that doctors are charging a bundle for nowadays. In fact, who knew that Quack-Quack would be such a trend-setter in the fashion department, too: *Cosmopolitan* magazine has actually suggested that we gals wrap our boobs in duct tape. Maybe magazine editors should stop flying to Milan for inspiration and start scouting out-patient mental facilities instead.

And if this isn't crazy enough, of course, there's now all this "celebrity beauty" craziness, too. Magazines devote whole sections to tracking down the brand of exfoliant used by Jennifer Love Hewitt. Cher gets her entire body renovated, Courtney Love buys herself a new nose, Britney Spears reportedly gets a boob job, and Joan Rivers's face has been reincarnated more times than the Dalai Lama. "Even I don't get up looking like Cindy Crawford," Cindy Crawford has said. And yet the media implies that these women are chronically, effortlessly, naturally beautiful—and that we can look just like them if we buy the same lip gloss and thigh cream as Cameron Diaz.

Wackier still, we gals are supposed to employ these "beauty secrets" to look as if we haven't done a damn thing to ourselves. Meanwhile, cosmetic ads refer to beauty as "a science," full of "breakthroughs," "patented" processes, and "state-of-the-art technology." And people accept these claims unquestioningly—even while they refuse to believe in evolution. *(Mascara? Sure, it's a science. But not Darwin.)* Go figure.

Now, you'd think we SmartMouth Goddesses would have a field day with this stuff, right? I mean, how ridiculous is a society that thinks it's nifty to inject botulism into our lips?

But for so many of us, unfortunately, beauty just ain't no laughing matter. It's our Achilles' heel—except that it's not just located in our feet, but in our hair, our face, and our body.

For all the "human progress" over the past two thousand years, we still feel an obscene amount of pressure to be beautiful. And we can all name the culprits: The media. Boys. Patriarchy. Capitalism. Calvin Klein. That moron in elementary school who insisted on weighing everybody publicly in gym class.

But frankly, some of the pressure to look beautiful is self-inflicted, too. Survey a bunch of us with XX chromosomes, and we'll tell you that we *like* to look stunning. We *like* to feel lithe and muscular, gorgeous and sexy. We *like* the "power" that beauty gives us. And we'll tell you that makeup is fun and that feminism means being able to do whatever we want with our faces and bodies, thank you very much.

Sure, we know that there *is* more, that there *should* be more, and that there *has* to be more to us than meets the eye. But this doesn't preclude us from wanting, on some level, to win the Miss Universe pageant, too.

Unfortunately, forces in our culture are only too happy to feed these longings and insecurities of ours—and inflate them to epic proportions like they do Cindy Crawford's breasts.

And so we women end up believing on some level that we're only beautiful if we're under forty years old and 110 pounds. We end up believing that, in order to be beautiful, we've gotta treat our bodies and faces like Humpty-Dumpty, delicately smashing them up and then trying to put them back together again—except better this time. (*Newsweek* has reported that an increasing number of average women—waitresses, nurses, students, and moms—are opting to spend our life savings on liposuction instead of on stuff like down payments for a home. We'd rather have fabulous abs for a few years than a financially secure future.)

We dissect and critique ourselves like a poultry inspector:

"Ugh, I hate my thighs. They rub together so much, it's a wonder sparks don't fly when I walk."

"Don't even get me started on my hair. In a third-world country, it would be harvested as a grain."

"The only thing that could improve my forearms at this point is a taxidermist."

Obviously, if we chicks are going to be seriously powerful in this world, we've got to learn how to appreciate our own natural, Goddess-given looks, to work with them as best we can, and then get over ourselves a little. Otherwise we'll just drive ourselves crazy.

Sure, this is far easier said than done. But let's think about something else for a moment: bungee-jumping.

Somebody has actually convinced folks that if they pay a guy one hundred and fifty bucks to tie a rubber band around their ankles and kick them off a suspension bridge, they'll have the time of their lives. Similarly, somebody has actually persuaded folks to buy John Tesh records. And somebody has actually persuaded folks that teaching a six-year-old to hunt with an assault rifle is a perfectly reasonable way to spend a Saturday afternoon.

So surely we gals can persuade *ourselves* to value beauty just a tad differently, no? Surely we can learn to love our looks without losing our life savings—or our minds.

How might we righteous babes withstand the barrage of beauty gar-bage? How might we begin our own *mental* makeovers?

1. **Remember: Famous beauties are just as miserable as the rest of us.** What do supermodels do all day? Stand still, shut up, and wear clothes. Ugh. These are probably my three least favorite things to do, short of getting root canal.

   Sure, famous beauties have starred in the fantasies of millions of pubescent boys, but just how difficult is *that* really?

   It's always assumed that celebrated beauties are happier and more loveable than the rest of us. I guess this is true. After all, Christie Brinkley has been married four times now. Jerry Hall married Mick Jagger, who publicly cheated on her for twenty years until announcing that, hey, guess what, honey, the wedding was bogus to begin with. Claudia Schiffer remained engaged for years to a guy who could make himself disappear at will, until the engagement broke off altogether. Marilyn Monroe's life was a succession of tragedies. Kate Moss checked herself into rehab . . . and *blah blah blah*. You get the idea.

   And then, on the other end of the spectrum, there are people like my friend Eliza, who's never been considered a "babe" in her life. What does Eliza have to show for her lack of pulchritude? A Harvard Ph.D, a kick-ass job heading one of the most prestigious news bureaus in the world, a big fat paycheck, a family that could smother you with love, a devoted circle of friends, and, oh yeah, a kind and gorgeous husband and a kid. So go figure.

   Next time we're tearing our hair out over our hair, it may help us to remember that beauty may attract attention and adoration from strangers, but it doesn't guarantee anyone love or happiness. And it certainly doesn't immunize us against the pain of being alive. For *that* we need a series of narcotics or a slot in the cryogenic freezer next to good ol' Walt Disney—neither of which, from what I understand, is terribly good for our looks.

2. **All life is not high school.** It's a feat unique to human nature that if we're called "warthog" or "dork-a-rina" for three years in high school, it can effectively abolish any sense of our own attractiveness for, oh, the next forty years. So it's important for us SmartMouth Goddesses to remind each other: Looks will never be as important as they are for those few years when we're all hormonally insane and have yet to pay income taxes.

Once we make it though the Wonderbra Years, we should find we have better things to do than go on grapefruit diets with our girlfriends or hang around a mall evaluating each other's hair, weight, and clothes. People who continue to adhere to the value system of high school after graduation are, frankly, pathetic. Sure, cheerleading squad is great exercise but not something we can put on a résumé. And unless we get pregnant during prom night, the shelf life of its importance is virtually nil.

Besides, nine times out of ten, anyone worth knowing later in life was generally miserable in high school. And in the workplace, nobody cares if we were a svelte homecoming queen or voted Most Beautiful. Nobody cares if we were called "warthog" or "dork-a-rina," for that matter, either. All they're interested in is stuff like money and vacations and not getting caught downloading porn from the Internet.

3. **If we cannot love our bodies, let's break both our legs.** My friend Sarah has recommended spending a few months in traction. Or in a wheelchair. She once spent an entire summer in a body cast after a bike accident. "Nothing, but nothing, in the world makes you appreciate your body so much as not being able to use it," she says. "You may hate your thighs now, but after they've been encased in plaster of paris and strung up over your head at a forty-five-degree angle for an entire summer, trust me: There will be nothing more beautiful than

seeing them bare again—especially if they still enable you to walk."

4. **Art museums beat *Vogue* any day.** Serious art is an amazing way to retrain our eyes to see beauty differently. Artists over the centruies loved to paint women of all sizes and all shapes. Granted, these artists were mostly white men, and so the women they painted were mostly white and naked, but their bodies and features were vastly different. And nobody, absolutely nobody, during the Renaissance painted Kate Moss.

5. **Bad hair days are inevitable and unavoidable.** And no matter what we do, bad hair days are largely out of our control. Ditto for the rest of our looks. Unless we're fabulous freaks of nature, chances are we'll have our goddess days and our god-awful days.

   Of course, the beauty industry would love to trick us into believing that a seventeen-dollar tube of "night creme" and some overpriced pseudo-European hair gel will actually enable us to *defy nature*, but c'mon: If someone truly had discovered a way to do this, wouldn't they have received the Nobel Prize already?

   Besides, we all know Murphy's Ugly Law of Beauty: No matter how hard we work to look breathtakingly gorgeous, the one day we run into our ex-lover is inevitably the day we've just had our wisdom teeth pulled and are staggering to the pharmacy in our sweat pants.

6. **Plastic surgery is fucking painful.** There's lots of money to be made convincing young women today that knives and needles are our best beauty tools. If we don't like something about ourselves, heck, we should just hack it off.

   These brilliant ideas are being promoted, of course, by the same people who, in a different time and place, would sound very much like Quack-Quack.

   Plastic surgeons are eager to convince us that a nose job, boob job, or cheek implants are as easy and harmless as, say, a makeover or a haircut. They have cute little computer programs that can morph our driver's-license photos into an *Esquire* cover in about three easy clicks.

Of course, this should tell us something right there.

Cosmetic surgery is not cosmetic. It is *surgery*. All the magical *before* and *after* pictures don't show people with their faces black and blue and swollen up like beach balls, or with their nipples cut off then stitched back on, their breasts bisected by scars. They don't show us all the painkillers we'll need to be on, or the risks involved with going under anesthesia.

If this isn't enough to repel us, checking out the doctors' offices might. I once went to a renowned ear, nose, and throat doctor for my allergies, and *apropos* of nothing, he informed me that I'd be a "real knockout" if I just had the tip of my nose "lifted a little." The guy wore wide-wale corduroys and had *duck pictures* hanging in his office. "Excuse me?" I wanted to say, "But if you really want to make the world more beautiful, why not start with your receding hairline and your Naugahyde couch?" Surgeons like him are making beauty decisions about people's faces throughout our country, and yet the majority of them can't even decorate a waiting room.

Our faces are each a unique work of art. I say we shouldn't let any doctor with the aesthetic sense of a walnut get his (or her) scalpel near us. In fact, shouldn't the arbiters of beauty in this world be great artists—not businesspeople or surgeons? (Then again, I guess if Picasso had been a plastic surgeon, he would have put both our eyes on one side of our nose . . .)

7. **Read the personals.** Ask straight women why we want to be beautiful, and many of us will eventually admit: "For men." "To be loved." "To get laid." "To get married."

From time immemorial, women have been taught that beauty is essential for attracting a mate. *Men are aroused by what they see*, we're told.

And yet, when it comes to men, we've also been told something else with equal fervency: *Men will fuck anything.*

So which one is it? Do we have to be beautiful, or will they fuck us anyway?

An informal survey conducted by yours truly reveals that, Goddess bless 'em, men are far more likely to fuck us anyway.

Yeah, it's true that a lot of guys out there are fixated on physical "ideals." But bless their filthy little hearts, what men consider "ideal" has a far greater range than we women give them credit for. Plenty of them like fleshy women, dark women, curvy women. They like bossy women, Christian women, redheads, dwarves. They're polymorphously perverse— they can fetishize anything and just about do! Just scan the personals and we can see: Their erotic imaginations know no bounds. A quick sample from *City Paper* in Washington, DC:

"SM seeks woman with pierced tongue."

"Large to small, if attractive and black, I'll kiss it all."

 "Seeking fit SF who doesn't look like Halle, Angela, or Zeta-Jones."

"This MBM is looking for the hairiest, hairy white woman. If you are a white woman with lots and lots of hair all over your body, call me."

I am not making these up.

So relax. Love and sex will come our way even if we're not a "great beauty." Whatever that means. Because for some guys, it means we've got one hairy, hairy back.

8. **Why should we really want to look like everyone else anyway?** Hey, the last man who truly wanted *all* women to look like Barbie was a squat, dark-haired guy with a toothbrush-bristle mustache. Had he been in America, of course, we would've laughed him off as a Charlie Chaplin impersonator. But he was in Germany—where the people have absolutely no sense of humor whatsoever—and so he was actually taken seriously and allowed to ruin much of the twentieth century. He just goes to show that the political and social impulse to make

everyone conform to a uniform standard of beauty is not a matter of aesthetics, or romance, or sexuality. It's fascism.

9. **And, finally, when all else fails, remember this:** As my grandmother used to say, Hey you're the one with the pussy. What are you knocking yourself out for? Let 'em get on their knees and beg.

Chapter 2

Skip the Spa. Viva Las Vegas!

Health: what my friends are always drinking to before they fall down.
—PHYLLIS DILLER

Recently, I saw some old World War II news clips about Germany. The grainy, black-and-white footage showed thousands of Nazi soldiers in identical uniforms goose-stepping through the streets in unison, thrusting their arms in the air and chanting "Heil Hitler!"

"Those people were insane," I thought. "Why would anyone surrender so mindlessly to a single leader like that?"

Then I went to my aerobics class.

Scores of women—dressed more or less identically—stepped in unison and thrust their arms in the air as an ex-cheerleader barked orders at them over the zombifying throb of Bananarama's "I'm Your Venus."

Face it: Jazzercise is fascism. It's not about strengthening your abs—it's about squelching your autonomy. Just try twirling like Twyla Tharp when you're supposed to be doing the box step. Move your left arm instead of your right. Do a bump-and-grind during the hip rotations and I promise: Within five minutes the instructor will be on your case. She will not be of the opinion that since it is *jazz*ercise, it might include a little improvisation. "Try to move with the group," she'll say curtly. Her voice will be like a stalk of sugar cane cracking across your back. High- and low-impact classes are "follow the leader" for grown-ups. Goose-step aerobics.

Is it any surprise that these classes have been designed primarily for women? Marketers aren't stupid: They know that men won't pay to have a Sadist in Spandex order them around for an hour (well, not in *public*, anyway . . .). When men work out, it's a celebration of control, strength, dominion. They whack their balls around with their squash racquets. They leap lithely around the basketball court and score.

They lift *free* weights. *We* obey Stair*masters.*

It's women who are more likely to spend our workouts skiing to nowhere, climbing to nowhere, pedaling to nowhere, running to nowhere on the treadmills, dutifully expending all our energies just to stay in place, doing the athletic equivalent of housework. Exercise, for many of us, contains an unwitting element of submission.

Don't get me wrong: I'm all for health and physical fitness. I'm all for women being strong and athletic. Yay for babes with biceps! Yay for sisters with stamina! Yay for low blood pressure! But too much of what passes for women's health today is really just a cocktail of consumerism, subjugation, and self-hatred mixed together and served up neat. Look what we're expected to swallow:

"Watch Your Mouth" warns *Shape* magazine.

"Soon both of you will be taking up less space," says a television ad for a portable treadmill (as if it's every woman's dream to be small enough to stuff away in a closet).

Health and "thinness," of course, are considered synonymous. In an ever-expanding world, where greatness and abundance are always placed at a premium—and people in power *throw their weight around*—women alone are supposed to get smaller, and this is supposed to be good for us. Ridiculous workout guides are placed side by side with twelve-hundred-calorie-a-day diets recommending that we subsist on grapefruit, tuna fish, or—my personal favorite— artificially flavored "health" milkshakes. "I drank Slim•Fast for twelve weeks and lost weight," say the people in the ads. Of course they did. They were starving.

Along these lines, *Health* magazine has suggested drinking fruit pectin with orange juice as a "natural alternative" to the dangerous diet drugs Redux and Fen-Phen. But drink fast, it warns: "Pectin quickly turns juice into jelly." Jelly? We're supposed to drink *jelly*? Meanwhile, *Self* magazine reports that botulism toxin can be injected into people to keep us from perspiring. I guess the reasoning behind that idea is that *dead people don't sweat . . .*

Maybe I'm silly, but I've always thought that activities that encourage suppression, passivity, obsessiveness, malnutrition, self-hatred, deprivation, and needless spending were, well, *un*healthy. Want to be of sound mind and body? Let's stop submitting to the tyranny of aerobics instructors, ab fascists, and calorie cops for a moment and consider the following instead:

1. **Complain.** Really bitch. Someone treats us badly? Let 'em have it. A burger isn't done the way we like it at a restaurant? Send it back. We've been overlooked for a promotion? Speak up. Whatever it is, let's not simper, whimper, whine, or rationalize it away. Let's raise hell, stand our ground, and let people know we're not happy. I am not kidding. Studies have shown that people who complain live longer. Yeah, there's always the possibility that this is because the people who have to listen to them die sooner, but who's to say?

   Too often, women don't speak up. We swallow our frustration and it turns into depression and tumors. Who needs that? Besides, the people who live the longest are invariably tough old bastards. Take my grandmother. She whacked men on the shin with her cane if they hogged the armrest at the movie theater—

and she lived to ninety-one. Want health and longevity? Be a pain in the ass.

2. **Do not calm down.** Practically every women's magazine I know has advised women to reduce stress by lighting candles, meditating, taking bubble baths, and "visualising a safe, nurturing place" whenever we get upset. Get quiet and get centered to get healthy, the mantra goes. While it's probably a good idea for us loud gals to mellow out once in a while, shutting up and getting "in touch with our feelings" has not, historically, been a problem for women. For centuries, we've been urged to be quiet, be still, think happy thoughts, and take various forms of tranquilizers. White women, at least, were also told to take to their beds as invalids and submit to hysterectomies in the name of preserving their health. Anybody sense an ulterior motive in this?

    If we're stirred up about something, chances are it's because there's a good reason. Let's blow out the candles, get up, get out, and take action. Ultimately, it will keep us happier and healthier than any narcotizing soak with Mr. Bubble.

3. **Masturbate.** (Or is it *Mistress*bate, arr, arr?) It certainly relieves more tension than a sixteen-dollar aromatherapy candle. Added bonus: subverts the patriarchy.

4. **Eat.** Have a nice bowl of chicken soup. Try a little bagels and lox while you're at it. Maybe some herring and a good slice of brisket. Jews did not survive two thousand years of persecution drinking wheat-grass juice. Neither will you.

5. **Let "avoidance" be our co-pilot.** Sticking our head in the sand can be a beautiful thing. Stay off the scale. When you get weighed at the doctor's, just turn your back to the numbers and tell the nurse not to share them with you. After all, if the number is high, you'll inevitably feel miserable. If it's low, you'll experience an absurd sense of ecstasy that is really better achieved lying down. Either way, one little instrument can render us manic-depressive. Who needs this? *We* know when we feel good.

Personally, I think the pharmaceutical companies are in cahoots with Jenny Craig. They want all of us to step on the scale every morning—that way, we'll be more amenable to spending the rest of our lives subsisting on Prozac and little frozen dinners premeasured like baby food.

To this end, why should we really read the fat and calorie counters on the sides of food packages, either? Unless we're diabetic, these things serve absolutely no useful purpose that I can think of. Because, face it: Once we're fondling a box of Oreos and holding it up close enough to read, chances are that we're going to eat them anyway.

6. **Boycott (excuse me, *Girlcott*) *Elle, Vogue,* and *Harpers' Bazaar.*** Consider it a mental-health measure. No woman has ever suffered from *not* seeing clothes she can never afford worn by models she can never look like.

7. **Our genitals are not Australia.** A few years ago, when my doctor, Jackie, was pregnant, she went for a checkup. Her ob/gyn said to her, "Okay, let me check you *down there.*"

   "*Down there?*" said Jackie. "What do you mean by 'down there'? You mean, like, Perth?"

   To this day, we fabulous females are still taught that our bodies are dirty, stinky, fussy, shameful—and that we should use deodorants "down there" that will make us smell like one of those little felt pine trees dangling from a rearview mirror of a taxi cab. As my grandmother would say, "fageddaboutit." Nature designed us to be like a self-cleaning oven. Any extra chemicals we spray on ourselves will only mess up our own delicate chemistry and damage the ozone layer, which, as we know, has already developed a hole—just about the size of Australia, in fact.

8. **Remember, we too could be in perfect shape if we earned six million dollars a year and worked out three hours a day.** Let's not be tricked by the media. Celebrities are in fabulous shape because they have inordinate amounts of

time, money, and help. Plus, it's their *job*. If we had a private chef cooking for us who'd originally founded a vegetarian spa in Switzerland, we too could maintain a low-fat, low-calorie, perfectly balanced gourmet diet for months on end. If we had a custom-made at-home gym, replete with a swimming pool, hot tub, and Nautilus machine—not to mention a three-hundred-dollar-an-hour personal trainer who came over four times a week and made sure our sorry ass was workin' it on the treadmill—we could look like the three Jennifers (Aniston, Lopez, and Love Hewitt) also.

9. **Go to Las Vegas.** I am not kidding. Yeah, Las Vegas is a city of tits 'n' ass, but it's also the perfect antidote to all the sexist stereotypes and expectations that are constantly imposed upon women. In Las Vegas, nobody cares how much you weigh. Nobody cares how you dress. Nobody cares what you look like, or how stylish you are, or how sexy you are, or whether you speak English. All the people in Las Vegas care about is money.

As long as we can afford the $4.99 all-you-can-eat buffet and have a few quarters to drop in the slot machine, the folks in Vegas are thrilled to wait on us hand and foot. And they'll do it with a smile—whether we're black, white, or yellow, whether we're male, female, or transgendered. As long as we're there to pay and play, Las Vegas doesn't discriminate.

Equally important, Vegas is cheap, and it's a city that wants us to relax and indulge ourselves. Nobody's wakin' us up at 6:00 A.M. to go on a sixteen-mile "nature walk" followed by a breakfast of buckwheat groats and a workshop on the importance of acidophilus. In Vegas, we can stay up all night, chow down on pancakes and prime rib twenty-four hours a day, wear gaudy clothing and comfortable shoes, get good and drunk with our friends, ride from casino to casino in a trolley, play a little fast-and-loose with our money, dance, scream, laugh, and flirt, and nobody will encourage us to do otherwise. This, to me, is far better for the heart and the soul than anything inside a vicious little gymnasium.

Chapter 3

૭૭

If You Can't Order Dessert, You Can't Ask for a Raise

---

*Food is an important part
of a balanced diet.*
—FRAN LEBOWITZ

Ugh. Women's relationship with food can be even more complicated than our relationship with our mothers. Strange as it may
seem, many of us feel we actually need *permission* to eat. Listen to a
group of us at a restaurant, and it's a Margaret Mead field day. More
often than not, one of four strange rituals will emerge: the justification, the confession, self-flagellation, or peer pressure.

With *justification*, a woman will actually present a prima facie
case for why she is ordering french fries. Take my friend Barbara:
"Well, I skipped breakfast today, then I walked to work, and all I had
was a Powerbar and a Diet Coke for lunch, and I'm getting a salad
with low-fat dressing, so I guess I can order the french fries, right?"

With *confession*, ordering french fries is a sin of such venal proportions, it requires penance before anything's even eaten. My friend Lauren: "Oh, my God. I am being *so* bad. I know I really shouldn't be doing this. I mean, french fries are like the worst thing for you. Augh. And I was so good all week. Okay. After this, you guys, I'm doing two hours on the Stairmaster. And I'm walking home. To Duluth."

Self-flagellation makes the direct link between ordering french fries and a fundamental character flaw. "I am such a pig. I am just, like, craving french fries," says my girl Inez. "What can I say? I am a *total* hog."

Peer pressure can actually work one of three ways. In the first scenario, a bunch of women will egg each other on to order the french fries—even while some opt for salads and mineral water. "Get the french fries! What's the big deal?" we'll laugh, eager and falsely dismissive, knowing full well that the person being goaded into breaking her diet is really a sacrificial lamb. If she orders the french fries, she'll enable the rest of us to feel superior for not giving in to *our* cravings, yet she'll also enable us to snatch fries off of her plate—or live vicariously by simply watching her eat them.

The second scenario is one in which women effectively cow each other into not ordering french fries through a sort of gastronomic sanctimony: "Now girls, we have to be good tonight," Shaniqua will announce. And then, well, who has the guts to be "bad"?

In the third scenario, we agree to mutually absolve each other of responsibility and guilt by ordering french fries as a *coalition*:

"Should we order some french fries?"

"Sure, let's get french fries!"

"Why not? Let's splurge! After all, it's Friday!"

Complicated, hm? The way we gals carry on about stuff like french fries, you'd think we were Hamlet. You'd think we were contemplating euthanasia. You'd think it was a career move. Military operations have been launched with less consideration than we give a menu.

And, perversely, many women feel more powerful when we're

in a state of self-denial than when we're ordering a plate of french fries—or even a lovely gourmet meal on a special occasion.

But if we can't bring ourselves to order dessert in a restaurant, how are we going to bring ourselves to ask for a raise?

Because, let's face it: Dieting does not exactly foster a sense of *entitlement*. It creates a mentality of self-criticism and scarcity. It makes us mean-spirited and defensive. It makes us see our daily lives in terms of limits, in terms of what we cannot and should *not* have.

Sure, it's good to be in shape and to eat nutritiously. But with the obsessive calorie-counting that goes on today, young women are apt to lose our sanity along with the pounds. Studies have shown that dieting reduces our ability to think rationally, to be organized, to feel compassion, and to focus on anything intensely other than food. Great.

If we gals want to pariticipate fully in our culture, we have a better shot at it with a full stomach. How can we study, forge successful careers, run businesses, and raise children well when we're hungry and preoccupied? To function well, women must eat well. And we must eat without shame, regret, or punishment. Eating is about many things, but it's also about *power*. To a majority of the world, which goes to bed hungry involuntarily, this is actually a no-brainer.

We all know that eating disorders in this country are epidemic. Girls are developing them younger and younger—and the disorders are now crossing over racial and ethnic lines, too. Approximately seventy percent of the female population is on a diet at any given time. More women diet than vote.

And yet, curiously, when eating disorders have been highlighted in the media lately, one of the responses from audiences has been: *yeah, well, dieting may be unhealthy, but it sure beats being a fattie. Heck, the majority of Americans are overweight!* It's as if there is no middle ground—or middle weight—between obesity and emaciation in America. No wonder young women only think in terms of size two or twenty-two: our culture's mind-set is that of an anorexic. It's as if size twelve doesn't exist.

Clearly, we need to develop a new attitude toward eating. Sure, it's a tall order, but so is a plate of french fries these days, and that's insane.

And so, here's some fresh food for thought, a little something to chew on, a different menu of choices and considerations.

1. **Women who eat are sexier.** Take it from Sophia Loren. "Everything you see I owe to spaghetti," she said.

   It's really no coincidence that sexual appetites and culinary appetites have always been linked, that the phrase "let yourself go" can refer to a babe who goes for broke at the buffet table *or* a sister who sizzles on the sofa.

   To a lot of guys, women who eat are simply more attractive. Says my friend David, "The sensuality of anorexia utterly escapes me." For years, skinniness in African-American communities was not considered sexy; it was viewed as a sign of illness or that women were "in a bad way."

   Besides, the way men see it, if a woman's comfortable putting one thing in her mouth, she'll probably be comfortable with another. Crude but true. Dinner, to them, is a preview of foreplay.

2. **Dieting displaces our ambition.** From the time we're little, we girls want gold stars and gold medals. But as Mary Pipher notes in *Reviving Ophelia*, at the exact moment when we're blossoming physically and developing intellectually, girls learn body hatred and get pressured into "dumbing ourselves down" to attract boys.

   So where does our ambition go? It gets turned inward, directed at "perfecting" our bodies; we strive to become the thinnest, the most virtuous at the dinner table, the "best little girl in the world." This is the dirty little secret that often gets buried in the national conversation about eating disorders. Yeah, anorexia and bulimia may be about control, insecurity, sexuality, abuse, and so on. But they're also about *competition*.

   "There was competition to be the sickest," a recovering

anorexic, Lisa Arnt, told *People* magazine in a 1999 cover story. "I always wanted to be the thinnest."

Eating disorders are a way to channel ambition and competitiveness—impulses that are often still not considered "feminine" and "attractive" in girls. For many of us, the first and only time we see women competing against each other in a sanctioned way is in the Miss America contest.

Yet we've got to realize that, ultimately, our so-called methods of self-control and self-improvement are self-defeating. All the drive and ambition we funnel into dieting could be better exploited. Never mind the fleeting sense of victory we feel turning down some cheesecake—we can experience far more glory and triumph by playing sports, starting a business, making the dean's list, or creating art. After all, there's no one less "winning" than a ninety-pound woman who has all the resources of the world at her fingertips but is too weak to reach for a Wheat Thin.

3. **Low-cal diets can leave us starved for friendship.** Since "thinness" puts us into an unspoken competition with other women, this also includes our friends. In dieting, we're always measuring ourselves against other women, seeing who's thinner, who's more virtuous at the dinner table. Time and again, women whisper to their lunch companions, "Am I thinner than that woman over there?" or "Oh, God, are my thighs as big as that?"

    As you may imagine, this doesn't do wonders for the female-bonding department. If we can't eat with a friend, chances are we can't really breathe around her either.

4. **Obsessions with food could bore us to death.** Recently, I went out for a celebratory dinner at an upscale restaurant with a group of women. Not one of us ordered an entree as it was printed on the menu: We requested the dressing on the side, the sauce on the side, the side dish as an entree, the entree downsized into an appetizer portion *but served as an entree*, the fish steamed instead of sautéed, and *yadda yadda yadda*.

Then, of course, when the food arrived, we immediately began discussing the merits of various diets (*The Zone* versus *Sugar Busters!*, carbs versus fats), how "good" or "bad" we'd been about working out that week, and how flabby we each felt. And sitting there—eating my grilled-not-sautéed salmon with the sauce on the side and extra steamed veggies instead of mashed potatoes—I started to feel my eyes rolling back into my head. It wasn't just the food boring me but my own conversation. Trekkies who spend their days translating the United States Penal Code into Klingon were probably more interesting to listen to than I was.

Chronic dieting is self-absorption taken to an art form. And, oh my Goddess, can it make us sanctimonious! Dieters are worse than people who've found religion: We have seen the Lite, and it is Weight Watchers' ranch dressing. There is absolutely no conversation in the world that's more unproductive and tedious than a bunch of healthy, generally well-fed young women sitting around complaining how fat we are. For the sake of nourishing our minds as well as our bodies, I say we've got to round out our meals *and* our girl talk. Otherwise, we risk nodding off into our steamed kelp—and suffocating.

5. **Women are starving in Africa, North Korea, the Balkans, and even the US.** Only the weak don't eat. For us gals in America, refusing to eat, glamourizing skinniness, and making self-denial a virtue is decadent and arrogant. We might as well voluntarily walk around in shackles and call it a fashion statement.

6. **Nobody gives a shit what we put on our plate.** Believe it or not, I still know women who refuse to be seen eating in public. They won't pile up a plate of hors d'oeuvres to bring back to their table of friends at a party, or they'll eat before a big date so that they won't have to order much at a restaurant. But, hey, trust me on this: When the guys check us out, they're not looking at our *food*. They're not saying, "See that girl over there, eating the focaccia with the olive dip instead of the low-

fat Baked Lay's?" or "Whoa, she just ordered the fettuccine alfredo *and* the fried-mozzarella appetizer." Nobody cares what we put on our plates except maybe (a) busybody, critical relatives, and (b) other obsessive, self-conscious dieting women.

So let's give it up, Girls, and eat freely when we're out. Women are starving in Africa, you know.

7. **If we can get our nails done, we can cook for ourselves.** So often I hear single women say, "Oh, I won't cook a nice meal if it's just for myself."

Sounds like they're auditioning to play a stereotypical Jewish mother: *Oh, don't mind me, sitting here alone. I'm not worth cooking for. I'll just reheat some rancid brisket left over from Mother's Day.*

I mean, what's wrong with a nice homemade meal *just* for ourselves?

We'll voluntarily plunk down fifty smackeroos to have some sadist in a beauty salon pour hot wax on our crotch and rip our pubic hair clean off our bikini line. But somehow, when it comes to eating dinner, we're not worth more time and effort than a Lean Cuisine?

Yeah, chicken marsala might require a little more work, but we deserve it at least as much as a bikini wax.

8. **Ice cream is nonpatriarchal.** Ice cream, frozen yogurt, milkshakes—every dairy product we can think of is the exclusive product of *females*. So, okay, they're cows. But eating this stuff can be a political act that neatly unites feminist principles with a love of animals. It can be our way of showing support for our bovine sisters! Fuck the vegans, I say. Anyone who doesn't eat ice cream for purely "ethical" reasons is a killjoy and a moron and ultimately not to be trusted. Pro–ice cream is pro-woman, Baby.

Okay, I admit this sounds a little stupid. But given the lengths to which we french-fry loving Freidas will go just to order a damn milkshake, such a rationalization certainly isn't much wackier than the rest. So let's have a nice piece of fish, a baked potato, and then maybe a bowl of Rocky Road for dessert. As my grandma used to say, "Once you're dead, you have the rest of eternity to be skinny. So why start now?"

Besides, no one ever conquered the world on an empty stomach.

Chapter 4

꩜

We Won't Shape History by Shaping Our Thighs

---

*Sure, beauty has the power to excite
men. But so does a box of donuts.*

I used to be a Big Sister to a seven-year-old girl who emigrated here from Mexico. Every week, I'd have lunch with her at her elementary school. We'd read books together, do art projects, and talk. When I first met her, she was just starting second grade. She was a good, enthusiastic student. "I want to grow up to be a teacher and a doctor," she told me proudly.

The next year, when she was in third grade, she announced she didn't want to be a teacher or a doctor anymore: She wanted to be a model.

"Why?" I asked.

"Girl power!" she shouted.

Oh, Dear Goddess, it starts so young.

A couple of years ago, *Time* magazine implied that women today care more about our bodies than our brains. In a much bally-hooed cover story, titled, "Is Feminism Dead?" the magazine claimed that women are too preoccupied with glamour and looks to engage in serious pursuits or politics of substance. The women's movement, it said, had degenerated into narcissism, into tell-all books about orgasms, and young women who equate "girl power" with the right to wear sequined culottes. "Feminism today is wed to the culture of celebrity and self-obsession," it declared.

Well, I thought, *if this is true, can you really blame us?* We're living in a culture where one of the richest, most powerful, and phenomenally successful women of all time—a television talk-show doyenne, movie star, and literacy goddess who has single-handedly built a multimillion-dollar production empire—has said in all seriousness that the most important accomplishment in her life has been to lose weight.

But that being said, I do think we gals would do ourselves *and* the little girls of the world a big favor by taking a step back for a moment and checking this reality.

Because the very same week that *Time* was painting us as narcissists, other significant pieces of news made the headlines, albeit in much smaller print. According to a census-bureau report, for the first time in history, more women than men ages twenty-five to twenty-nine are earning college and graduate degrees, and these degrees enable us pull down at least forty percent more income than our high school–educated sisters. Higher education also makes a bigger difference in women's salaries than in men's, particularly now. According to reports, the Information Age has created such a demand for brainiacs that a Smarty Pants can often write her own ticket.

Yeah, our culture is increasingly visual, but it's the women *behind* the cameras and computers who are best poised to reap its goodies. The glamourous fantasies touted in the pages of *Vogue* and *Vibe* are just that: fantasies. In reality, we gals have a far better shot at striking it big as a software developer or as a Webmistress than as an actress, model, or singer.

If we want to be truly subversive and powerful, we'd be wise to embrace our inner geek—and to actively encourage our younger sisters, daughters, and nieces to do the same. We gotta celebrate that cerebellum! Get down and get bookish! Sure, geeks may not have the sex appeal of, say, Salma Hayek, or, ahem, the exposure of Pamela Lee, but if we want to have a stake in the twenty-first century, nerdhood is the way to go.

For the first time in history, women in America outnumber the men at universities, and for the first time in history, we have the chance to make it in any field, from aerospace engineering to zoology. Yet, curiously enough, we're still being encouraged to value our *looks* more than our *minds*—perhaps more so now than twenty years ago, when MTV wasn't beamed into millions of living rooms and fashion models reflected twenty-three percent of the female population, not six.

A prevailing message in our culture is that women can't possibly be intelligent and desirable at the same time. Watching Velma and Daphne on a rerun of *Scooby-Doo* . . . or Blaire and Natalie on *The Facts of Life* . . . or even MTV's brilliant and ironic *Daria,* we don't have any trouble picking out the smart girls. They're the short, fat ones; the witty ones: the ones with glasses and no dates. And, of course, the cute girls are all popular and about as deep as toilets.

Were I not such a Pollyanna, in fact, I'd wonder if there wasn't some sort of cultural conspiracy at work. For as Naomi Wolf pointed out in her book *The Beauty Myth*, thinking obsessively about fat and dieting has actually been shown to change people's thought patterns and brain chemistry. A preoccupation with looks, then, has the potential to short-circuit women's intellects—precisely at a time when education and brain power are at a premium in the marketplace.

If we gals could stop focusing so much on our looks and start redirecting that energy toward our minds instead, we'd create even more serious competition in the job market. We'd earn more moolah and play a bigger role in shaping our society than we do now. And we'd probably put some of the multimillion-dollar beauty and diet companies out of business. And then, Goddess knows, the Earth would fall off its axis.

Of course, attempts to disparage women's intelligence are hardly revolutionary. Brains and femininity have been placed on a crash course with each other throughout history. In the Middle Ages, the only way most girls could receive an education was by joining a nunnery. During the Renaissance, while da Vinci was drawing up plans for a flying machine, enterprising midwives were being burned at the stake as witches. When Western women in the nineteenth century began making a name for themselves as popular novelists, they were derided as "scribbling women." In 1873, a Dr. Edwards Hammond Clark published *Sex in Education*, in which he argued that education is harmful to women because mental activity draws blood away from our reproductive organs. In 1905, a psychologist named G. Stanley Hall asserted that specialized professional work was "alien to the female mind." In the 1950s, a pamphlet about how to identify a lesbian was published. One of the dead giveaways of dykedom? A woman reading a book.

And perhaps most tellingly, just a few years ago, the women of Mensa posed for *Playboy*. Why? Apparently, the women felt the need to show the world that they were more than a bunch of high IQs. *More than a bunch of high IQs?* Zoiks! I'm sorry, but we SmartMouth Goddesses have got to question any culture where a woman feels compelled to take off her clothes in order to prove that, *really, she's more than just a mathematical genius.*

For all the talk about women's empowerment today, there are still few celebrated images of women who are intellectual. We're still not really brought up to see ourselves as powerful or heroic except in ways that are sexualized. Even female superheros like Wonder Woman and Xena look fabulous in a bustier. Even Buffy is way buff.

Ironically, Camille Paglia, who insists that women's greatest powers lie in our beauty and sexuality, has obtained her greatest power through the academy. I can't help but wonder how successful Ms. P. would've been if she'd spent her career in a beauty salon instead of in a library.

Besides, if women's greatest power really is our beauty and sexuality, well, then, I say we demand a refund. Because for centuries we've subscribed to all sorts of nonsense in the name of "enhancing" our "feminine powers." Be it foot-binding, wearing enormous brass rings around our necks, or getting silicone balloons implanted in our chests, we have relentlessly mutilated ourselves in pursuit of our "womanly power." And what has it gotten us? Better overall pay? A political voice? Help with the laundry?

For that matter, what has it gotten the world? Has it abolished racism, or brought about peace, or even shortened the lines for the ladies' rooms? Sure, beauty *does* have the power to excite men, but so does a box of donuts. I mean, can't we aspire to something a little loftier—and with a little more shelf life?

Only one woman's beauty has truly changed the course of Western history, and that was Helen of Troy, whose face started a war. Thousands of people were killed, and today nobody has the faintest idea what she looked like.

Cleopatra was apparently beautiful, too, but she was also highly educated and spoke seven languages. How likely is it that Marc Antony would have fallen for her if she sat across from him in Alexandria twirling her hair around her finger and giggling?

And since we're flipping through history, what about the Virgin Mary? Maybe it's inappropriate to ask but, hey, does anybody know if she was a hottie?

No woman's beauty has ever outlived her, with the possible exception of Marilyn Monroe, and that's largely because Andy Warhol turned her face into wallpaper. And as Norma Jean reminds everyone, beauty may get you into bed with a couple of Kennedys, but it won't bring you happiness, or marriage, or children, or respect, or love.

The women who have truly influenced the world have done so because of their conviction and smarts. Jane Austen, Harriet Tubman, Marie Curie, Shirley Chisholm, Helen Keller—none of these women made an impact because they were the bomb in a bikini. Even Anne Frank and Joan of Arc, who were teenagers, didn't make history because they had perky little boobs.

Millions of lives have been saved because of Clara Barton, who founded the Red Cross. Margaret Sanger, who pioneered birth control, has done more to liberate women sexually than Madonna. Rosa Parks didn't get invited to a lot of glitzy Hollywood parties, but her effect on history surely exceeds that of, say, Gwyneth Paltrow. As far as I know, Sojourner Truth never wore hot pants. Ditto for Margaret Mead. Mother Teresa was not exactly a "10" in the looks department. And neither was Golda Meir. And neither was Eleanor Roosevelt, arguably the most important woman of the twentieth century.

Thirty women so far have won the Nobel Prize, in physics, chemistry, physiology and medicine, literature, and peace. Does anyone have a clue what any of these women look like?

Even in twentieth-century American pop culture, the majority of famous women who have had real staying power and influence are not classical "wispy beauties." Mae West, Lucille Ball, Barbra Streisand, Bette Midler, Roseanne, and, yes, Oprah Winfrey, have been smart as hell and multitalented. In the long run, their brains have served them better than their sex appeal. And it'll serve *us* well to remind each other of this from time to time.

Sure, it's important to be healthy and feel good in our own skin. And it's hard for young women to overcome the pressures and the values that are foisted upon us, especially in high school and college. Ironically, in school—which is supposedly ground-zero for intellectual pursuits—looks are often the primary form of social currency. And, sure, sexy and glamourous stuff is, well, sexy and glamourous (hey, I read *In Style*). But my own egotistical little heart wants all of us gals—young and old—to aspire to being more than the flavor of the month, or a Spice.

If physical appearance is what we women idealize the most, it'll undermine our chances for serious, enduring, historic achievement. We've got to remember (and, if need be, *rearrange*) our priorities here. Our gray matter has far greater staying power than our thighs ever will; it has the capacity to endow us—and the world— with joy, enlightenment, and influence well into our old age. So why focus so much on shaping our bodies when we can shape history? Let's say it loud, proud, and repeatedly to every chick we know: Real girl power lies between our ears.

Chapter 5

ൟ

Niceness: Barf

It's the good girls who keep diaries.
The bad girls never have time.
—TALLULAH BANKHEAD

Okay, let's start with a quiz. Who do you like better: Rosie O'Donnell or Kathie Lee Gifford?

If you're reading this book—which presumably means you have taste—you, like me, chose Rosie. Hands down. And presumably you understand, too, what I mean when I say that it's better to be fabulous than to be "nice." Yeah, both Rosie and Kathie are considered nice, but Rosie is nice as in "kind," whereas Kathie is nice as in "a sanctimonious goody-goody."

In our culture, people tend to be valued for being inspiring and entertaining. With perhaps the notable exception of some morning-show hostesses, people are rewarded for being bold and inventive. For being assertive, funny, and individualistic. For having a bit of an edge.

Yet, when it comes right down to it, women are still encouraged to be, above all else, capital-*N* "nice." We learn that it's more important to be nice than to be interesting. It's more important to be nice than to be ourselves. It's certainly more important to be nice than to keep it real.

Nice might be "nice," but c'mon.

First of all, as we brazen, down-'n'-dirty gals know: Nice is usually not nearly nice enough. I mean, just look at our girl Kathie Lee. Tell me she's not the queen of passive-aggression. Nine times out of ten, "perfect good girls" like her live in a straightjacket fabricated out of appearances—and, boy, does that make them resent the hell out of the rest of us. And so they wind up using their niceness as a cudgel: They bludgeon us with their perfection—*see how good I am, see how great my kids are, see how dreamy my marriage is. See how my casserole doesn't leak over the sides of the Tupperware*. Ugh. It's enough to make you want to get puking stinking drunk, if only so that you can throw up on them.

Second, niceness alone just doesn't get a gal that far. Kathie Lee herself has got to know this. It took a lot more than fresh breath and good white teeth to get where she is today. Those million-dollar incisors better be damn sharp, too.

Interestingly, throughout the 1990s, Republicans insisted that political races should be about "character." They elevated character to an "issue." The problem, however, was that the Republicans confused character with virtue—with being a close-minded, sniggling, sanctimonious do-gooder.

In trying to present himself as a "man of character," Dan Quayle actually bragged that he had the same moral beliefs that he'd had twenty years ago.

He was *proud* of this? Hell, I wouldn't brag about having the same *haircut* as I did twenty years ago, let alone the same belief system. And I certainly wouldn't vote for anybody who did.

Well, as we've all learned, Americans aren't really interested in character in terms of *virtue* or *niceness*. We're interested in character in terms of *personality*. We're a country that prefers Scarlett to

Melanie and Rhett to Ashley. We like our leaders large, colorful, mythic, entertaining. We're not nearly so compelled by leaders *having* character as by their *being* one. As in a *cartoon*. The right wing may think America should be governed by the equivialent of Saint Francis of Assisi, but most of us are happier casting our ballots for the political equivalent of, say, Foghorn Leghorn.

Why else would people have voted for Ronald Reagan? Or Sonny Bono? Or Jesse "the Body" Ventura? Why else would people prefer Bill Clinton to Al Gore? "Gore is boring," people whined. Meanwhile, my grandmother voted for Clinton precisely *because* he ate pussy and jogged to McDonald's. "Hey, he's as horny, hungry, and morally inept as the rest of us," she said. "I like that guy."

Face it, if we really cared about character in terms of traditional virtue—if we really wanted our politicians to be goody-goodies—Mister Rogers would be president. But on some level, we know: niceness alone doesn't cut it.

And yet, here we women are: still striving to be pleasing, sweet, cheerful, agreeable—we're still hoping to get voted Most Likeable, even though that stuff won't get us into the White House.

All the supposedly racy, "modern" women's magazines are filled with articles on: "Want to up your like-ability?" "Do you make your lover feel loved?" "Are you a good friend?" "Ten tips toward being a better co-worker." The underlying premise is that, above all else, women should strive to be good and nice and pleasing.

"Good girls" are accommodating and giving. Good girls don't hurt other people's feelings. Good girls are not overly "aggressive," competitive, or boastful. Good girls please others. But what good girls are good *for* is a good question. I mean, it's one thing to be decent; it's another to be a doormat.

Ironically, just as the right wing of the Republican party staked out virtue as part of its ideological territory, traditional feminism did little to truly liberate women from what Naomi Wolf once called "the dragons of niceness."

And let me tell you: Wolf has had trouble slaying these "dragons of niceness" herself. I once attended a lecture she gave at the

University of Michigan where she actually said—I am not making this up—that women shouldn't make penis jokes.

No penis jokes?

Apparently it's okay for us to practice self-deprecating humor, or even to chide men in a ladylike, giggly, bell-tinkling, really-we-don't-mean-it kind of way. But by all means, no laughing at the Staff! No fooling about the Tool! No jokers about the Pokers, or hecklers about the Peckers! No hee-hees about the Pee-pees, please! Those little fleshy appendages attached to men that go up and down of their own accord are *serious* body parts. Good girls and friendly feminists *shouldn't* laugh at them. It isn't nice, Wolf said. We'll alienate people.

Yeah, well: no penis jokes, my ass.

Look, if there's one thing that can truly unite women—that can cut across all racial, ethnic, religious, and class lines—it's a good penis joke. You wanna make a roomful of women crack up? Just roll your eyes and say "penis." In fact, this probably works in a roomful of men, too. Penis jokes are crowd pleasers: Why else does everybody watch *Friends*? Besides, take away a woman's right to laugh about anything, including penises, and in my book you're no longer entitled to say with a straight face that you are pro-choice.

But Wolf is hardly alone. While feminism may have freed women's bodies from bras, laws, and oppressive morals, it has also helped stuff our personalities into the girdle of Political Correctness and the corset of Victimhood—both variations of the Tyranny of Niceness.

For example, oodles of feminist theorists have claimed that men are inherently violent (i.e., scum), while women are inherently peaceful (i.e., nice). And I've got to admit that when I was in college, I agreed with this wholeheartedly. After all, it was the guys who were playing paint-ball, date-raping women, getting crazy drunk, and throwing sofas out the window. Meanwhile, what were we gals doing? Sitting around the womyn's center, sipping herb tea, and talking about how men were suffering from testosterone poisoning.

It's so easy to buy the feminist rap that "men are naturally aggressive, women are naturally nurturing"—especially because, hey, in this scenario, we win! We're *nicer*! Sounds great, right?

That is, until someone grabs our ass on the street, threatens our children, or burglarizes our home. Then we see how "inherently peaceful," "nurturing," and "nonviolent" we really are. Then we see where self-righteous niceness gets us. Then we see how claiming the moral high ground as our chromosomal birthright is like volunteering to spend our life in a playpen.

Funny, but for all our supposed man-hating, bra-burning, radical, hairy-legged rage, a lot of mainstream white feminists have really been uncomfortable with anger and assertiveness. These qualities have been portrayed as "inherently male," implying that women who exhibit them are somehow unfeminine and not nice. When it comes right down to it, a lot of feminists I know prefer their personal politics wrapped in a doily, tied with a bow. They prefer that "everybody play nice."

At past Holly Near concerts, I've seen the audience holding hands and singing sweetly, in harmony, "We are gentle, angry people. And we are singing, singing for our lives."

Oh, right. Like singing is really going to keep us from getting sexually harassed? Try singing to a pervert. Better yet, to a tank. And let's not kid ourselves: We can be gentle. And we can be angry. But usually not at the same time.

Most of the women's events and feminist functions I've attended are so sugary, in fact, they could give you diabetes. The participants are constantly going around in circles, discussing our feelings about the event, our feelings about each other's feelings about the event, our "issues" with each other's issues about our feelings about the event. Oh, my Goddess—there's so much touchy-feeliness, it makes you want to clobber somebody with a Birkenstock. And everyone gets a turn to speak, everything is done by consensus, everyone is praised for speaking, everyone is praised for praising each other. As my girl Ophi once said, "There's so much ass-kissing at those events, they should hand out ChapStick at the door."

Yeah, civility is important. Ditto for democracy. And inclusion. And respect. And certainly, kindness and compassion are crucial in this brutal world. But *niceness*? Niceness can be fascist in its own way. When a movement is run as if it's orchestrated by Miss Manners, the underlying message becomes that it's more important for women to accommodate everyone, and to be *nice* to everyone, and to worry about not offending anyone, than it is to be effective or truthful. It winds up reinforcing the idea that women should behave like good girls. And in doing so, it constrains us just like everything else. It's not much different from our fourth-grade teacher telling us to lower our voice and play nice. Or our parents telling us not to say we hate our peas: *Good girls don't talk that way*.

Is it any wonder that there's been a backlash? That we've got Camille Paglia lobbing verbal grenades at feminism? Or Alanis Morissette's edgy, rage-filled albums going platinum? Or Elizabeth Wurtzel, posing shirtless and giving the world the finger on the cover of a book that praises "difficult women," including a teen adulteress who shot a housewife in the face? Or cult adoration for Gwen Stefani singing "I'm just a girl," while she karate kicks around the stage, flexes her muscles, and revels in teasing and humiliating the boys?

Nowadays, it seems, we gals are presented with two idealized modes of behavior. We can either be nice or nasty, a pussycat or a bitch. Ironically, the same dichotomy that used to apply to our sex lives now applies to our personality. We stand to be cast—or to cast ourselves—as either Katie Couric *or* Katie Roiphe. Courtney Cox *or* Courtney Love. Yech.

In the long run, of course, neither choice serves us well. We shouldn't really have to choose. Most of the greatest, most enduring women of our culture are hybrids. Take Mae West. Barbara Jordan. Eleanor Roosevelt. Julia Child. Molly Ivins. Queen Latifah. They're complicated women. They're not afraid to be strong, rich personalities. And they're not afraid to be "not nice."

Beyond everything else, these women have got personality. They've got chutzpah. Sometimes they're brash. Sometimes they make mistakes. Not everybody adores them—and they don't really give a shit if everyone does. But their appeal has endured—and in certain cases their words, work, and influence have outlived them.

Why? In part, because they refused to be constrained or confined to the roles of either a good girl or a bitch. They've had the courage to be themselves.

So if you're ever feeling cowed or self-conscious—if you worry about what people will think of you or whether you're not being nice—think about the power and the importance of cultivating your own personality and keepin' it real.

And if this doesn't help, hey, think about all the reasons Rosie O'Donnell leaves Kathie Lee Gifford in the dust.

Rosie has a big fresh mouth and a big fresh heart. And while she became the new queen of daytime largely because she was the Queen of Nice, nobody in the audience ever kids themselves. We all know that if Rosie gets good and pissed—say, about the NRA— hey, she's from *Noo Yawk*. She's going to tell you exactly what she thinks. She's not going to get all passive-aggressive and manipulative or simpering on your ass. Girlfriend's got an edge. She is nice but she is tough, too. More to the point, she's true to herself, thank you. And that's what makes her—as it makes any of us gals who are true to ourselves—far more likeable, and genuinely nicer in the end, than that waffle-topping Kathie Lee.

Chapter 6

໖໖

PMS Is a Power Tool

---

*Why harangue our loved ones when we
can harangue our legislators?*

Recently, my friend Jerome told me that, while he's certainly "not a sexist or anything," he thinks that sometimes women "exploit PMS" as an excuse for bad behavior.

Yeah, right.

I told him the real problem is that we women don't exploit PMS nearly enough.

I've always thought it was pretty funny that, for years, we gals were told that PMS was "all in our heads" by a medical profession that tended to view every other ailment that plagued us as the product of our uteruses. And now that PMS *is* taken seriously, men use it to question our ability to think rationally. This from a gender that regularly attends Monster Truck Expos.

Of course, if a guy has raging hormones, no one considers it a threat to his competency. But for centuries, those of us who have a womb for rent have been deemed naturally "hysterical." Our reproductive organs have been considered our sole source of identity and destiny—despite the fact that men can, if permitted, talk nonstop about nicknames for their penises for an average of twenty-seven years.

So here's what I think we should do when it's That Time of the Month. Rather than ride our hormonal upheavals like a mechanical bull, or even try to assuage them, I think we should exploit the hell out of them to combat sexual discrimination. Practice some "directed PMS." Some Estrogen Activism. Some Progesterone Power. Let's harness those mood swings, milk those menstrual cramps, let our ovaries, ahem, egg us on, and focus our frustrations for all that they're worth.

Every day, we chicks are subtly pressured into being seen and not heard, into denying what we want, into tempering our rage, ambition, sexuality, and appetites. Yet each month Mother Nature turns up the thermostat in our own little incubator until we can't help but behave like a force of nature ourselves. We're chemically compelled to weep, bitch, emote, scream, laugh, eat, and make love with abandon. We devour that bag of chocolate-covered pretzels; we curse out the guy who tries to cut in front of us at the line at the Jiffy Lube; we pull our lover into the bedroom as if our libido has just declared a national state of emergency.

Despite whatever social constraints have been placed on us, we're hormonally programmed to defy them anyway.

Talk about a natural resource!

So I say we SmartMouth Goddesses use this to the Max.

Whenever our breasts get achy, let's use it as a time to really get something off our chests. Let's direct our frustration, rage, and passion toward a greater end; let's use them constructively, productively, and politically. Next time our hormones heat up and we feel like chewing out our roommate because he bought the wrong kind of fucking mayonnaise, here's what I say we do instead: Take it out on the federal government.

I mean, why harangue our loved ones when we can harangue our legislators? After all, that's what we pay them for: It's their *job* to listen to our concerns.

The White House actually has its own "public complaint line," (202) 456–1000, plus e-mail addresses for the Prez, the Veep, and the Grand Dame herself (they're at, respectively: president@white-house.gov; vice.president@whitehouse.gov; and first.lady@white-house.gov).

Or, better yet, let's contact the folks in Congress (for your representative, go to www.house.gov; for your senators, go to www.senate.gov). They don't hear from us hot menstrual mamas nearly enough, and they need to know that we're upset and paying very close attention.

Let's let 'em feel the full bulk of our fury about something that's legitimately bothering us about the world at large—say, gender inequities in health-care research, the pathetic amounts of parental leave in this country, or the fact that many American-based multi-national corporations pay fewer taxes than our aunt Marie.

And why stop there? For those five days each month when we've been hormonally hijacked, there are women's health clinics to be defended, underpaid amigas at Mickey D's to be organized, and redwood trees to be protected. I mean, which is ultimately more satisfying: picking a fight with our S.O. or telling some Focus on the Family lunatic just where he can stick his giant plastic fetus?

Besides, lots of us gals today feel kind of *blah* about activism: Either we're cynical or sick of all the "Kumbaya" singing or we simply have too many other things on our plate. But PMS provides us with a regular, ready-made desire to vent. So if we set aside That Time of the Month to routinely engage in our own little, ahem, political bloodletting, we can collectively become a force to be reckoned with—with minimal effort on our part. Speaking out just becomes part of our once-a-month to-do list. You know: *Buy Tampax. Take Motrin. Contact Congress with Complaint of the Month. Eat half pound of M&M's and some pickle slices . . .*

If we've got to endure a so-called curse, then let's inflict one on the very folks whose salaries we pay and whose job it is to represent our interests and improve this crazy world.

No doubt some dimwits like my friend Jerome will tell us that such ideas are irrational. So be it. Just remember: As women, we have the Goddess-given gift of getting good and pissed off every month—and we're not about to squander it.

Then we can tell them to shut the fuck up and pass us those chocolate-covered pretzels.

Chapter 7

಄

Your Clitoris as Disneyland

---

*If God hadn't wanted us to touch
ourselves, he would've made our
arms shorter.*

—GRANDMA

You know, men rarely get more creative than when it comes to devising euphemisms for playing with themselves. Ask Joe Sixpack to describe masturbating and suddenly he's a poet. He's William Shake-the-spear. "Jerking off?" he says. "Oh, that's easy. How about flogging the bishop? Choking the chicken. Boxing Goofy till he pukes. Polishing the knob. Stroking the salami. Doing the one-fisted tango. Glad-handing with Mr. Happy. Hoo boy," he gasps. "Just talking about it is giving me a doggie boner. Time to go slap the dachshund."

But women, what do we say? "Playing the skin flute" isn't exactly a term of self-endearment for us. Ditto for "spanking the monkey." I mean, *really*. We don't have pet phrases for masturbating because, as we all know, it's not something we're supposed to *do*, let alone talk about.

When I was in high school, two guys from my class used to shout across the hallway to each other: "Hey, Mark, what're you doing tonight?"

"I dunno, Biff. Watching the playoffs and jerking off, I guess."

The fact that I still remember this charming little exchange shows how much it astonished me. I mean, would you ever hear two sixteen-year-old girls joke:

"Hey, Gabi, what're you up to this afternoon?"

"I don't know, Suze. I thought I'd go home, watch *General Hospital*, and switch on the electric boyfriend for a little while."

Don't think so.

In high school, most of us gals would sooner suffer the humiliation of going to the prom with our parents than admit to masturbating. Even the word sounded low-life to us. Ironically, while sticking our fingers down our throats was considered perfectly acceptable (even a badge of honor among some) sticking our fingers down our *pants* was certainly not. I mean, *Eeeww. That* was just gross. You might as well be sticking your fingers up your nose.

Never mind that we were constantly and eagerly exchanging graphic details about our sexual escapades with *other* people. I went to one sweet sixteen where a bunch of us, drunk on (what else?) pink Champale, compared flavored condoms as if they were Bonne Bell Lipsmackers. We thought nothing about discussing blow jobs or tittering about how some guy's penis was shaped like a croissant. (*"I mean, it looked like it should come with a cup of coffee and a packet of jelly!"*) But self-stimulation? *That* we equated with being "dirty," oversexed, and pathetic. Go figure.

For all our sexual hipper-than-thouness, none of us ever stopped to examine our Orwellian, so-called logic. Like everyone else our age, we assumed if you satisfied yourself, you were "desperate." If you got off *without* a guy, you were "slutty." And if you understood and enjoyed your own anatomy, you were a "pervert."

The sexual revolution didn't do much to stem the tide of messages we received about *self-contained* sexuality: We still believed that girls aren't supposed to "do it" with ourselves. Our bodies are to remain "hands-off"—even if the hands are our own. Orgasm and sex are things that are "done" to us, that "happen" to us, that we "surrender" to. On our own, we're divorced from sexuality; we're "allowed" to marry it only through a man.

We accepted these contradictions unquestioningly, the same way we accepted all those ridiculous advertisements instructing us to make sure we had that "fresh all day, feminine feeling." (Whatever the hell *that* meant. One of my friends once actually used feminine-deodorant spray on her armpits.) And if we had a fair dose of traditional religion growing up, well, that just complicated things even further. As a friend of mine put it: There's nothing quite like the possibility of burning in hell to put the kabash on enthusiastic self-love.

It was only after we got to college that the women I knew began to discuss "petting the kitty." And then it was only at late-night rap sessions with a lot of Kahlua and chocolate plying our tongues: "Oh, my God, I just discovered the joys of a hand-held shower massage," my roommate confessed one night, and all of us started giggling, half knowingly, half with relief.

Then the floodgates were open. The veil of embarrassment lifted—and there was no stopping us. Once it was clear we were all members of Autoerotics Anonymous, we couldn't shut up. We began trading "recipes."

"Read a book called *For Yourself.* Or *My Secret Garden.*"

"Forget the books. Get yourself a vibrator. I borrowed my aunt Mathilda's one night. I came so many times, I almost blacked out."

"I'm having a love affair with my bathtub. Just lie under the faucet and let the water do all the work. You can come two or three times without lifting a finger. It's like, Look, Ma! No hands!"

Recently, pop-culture references to women masturbating have started to come out from under the covers, so to speak—especially when there's been a cigar and a president involved. And every time I've caught one—whether it's a rap song by the righteous T-Boz, or an episode of *Sex and the City* in which one of Carrie's crew gets addicted to a Hitachi Magic Wand, or Nastasha Lyonne dancing with a vibrator in the movie *The Slums of Beverly Hills*—I've felt a little thrill and relief. Finally it's being acknowledged!

For, Goddess knows, we gals could benefit from a little less cultural shame. Despite the commercial raciness of *Cosmo* or the dreary honesty of *Our Bodies, Ourselves*, a lot of us still feel a glint of embarrassment about masturbation, even in the privacy of our own bedrooms, let alone in conversation.

Yet, ironically, there's one group who's *dying* to hear women talk about jerking off: straight guys. I am not kidding. Tell a straight guy that you gave yourself an orgasm and it's almost as good as telling him that you and your gorgeous twin sister used to play doctor together. Tell a straight guy that you're happy to make yourself happy, and he's transported to Fantasy Island. He can't hear enough about it. He wants all the pornographic details. He is awed. He is reverent. He is *grateful*. He actually shuts up and *listens*.

Stunningly, it never seems to dawn on him that, just like with the lesbians he fantasizes about, the fact that you can be satisfied without him actually *decreases* his chances of joining in the fun. *Oh, please, tell me more*, he begs. *Do you do it like in the movies, wearing high heels and a garter belt?*

A few years ago, I had a surreal conversation with three nineteen-year-old guys at the University of Michigan.

"We're all dying to date this one girl on our hall," they told me. "She told us she *masturbates*."

"And this makes her attractive *how?*" I asked.

"Because!" they practically shouted. "Don't you get it? Any girl who masturbates has got to be a total hottie."

Well, hey. If this is all it takes to get boys excited and interested, it sure beats plucking our eyebrows or wearing a "body slimmer." But more to the point, I think, is the fact that taking matters in our own hands, ahem, gives us more power in the long run—and *not* because it gets the guys' knickers in a twist.

It's certainly the only time-honored pleasure that won't get us pregnant, give us STDs, clog our arteries, land us in jail, become addictive, raise our blood pressure, or run up our credit-card bills. Talk about good clean fun.

It's also a great way to get rid of menstrual cramps, tension headaches, and insomnia. (Though in college, a lot of us found it really reenergized us if we had to pull an all-nighter, too.) Hell, it even burns calories. And if we like to use a toy or two when we play, why, we're even helping the economy.

One could argue that it's good for the old mental health. Back in the nineteenth century, vibrators were actually prescribed for women suffering from "hysteria." Granted, I'm not one to put much stock into the theories of Victorian medicine. But if a woman is getting all bent out of shape because the world is pushing her buttons, telling her to lie back and push her own for a while certainly ain't a bad idea.

True, the Catholic Church, among others, does think we'll burn in hell for it. But look at it this way: In the Middle Ages, the Church also opposed using forks.

But beyond all that, treating our clitoris as Disneyland is also a form of self-education.

Recently I spoke with psychologist Harriet Lerner, author of the book *The Dance of Anger*. For two decades, Lerner has been trying to "raise vulva consciousness." Why?

"Most parents still raise their kids with some variation of 'boys have a penis and girls have a vagina,'" she says. "To this day, most parents continue to say 'vagina' when they mean 'vulva.' Many educated parents report that they have never heard the word 'vulva'—including a large number who think the term refers to a Swedish automobile."

(Oh, great.)

Such misinformation breeds confusion, to say the least. As Lerner notes, "It's extremely disorienting and shaming to girls to discover a major source of pleasure on the outside for which there is no name, which doesn't exist."

It's no surprise then that a friend of mine who worked on a women's health project found that women who don't touch their bodies are often clueless about them. Some women don't even know that the urethra—where we pee from—is separate from the vagina. Some girls are going through the *Kama Sutra* page by page with their boyfriend but don't have the slightest idea about how to have an orgasm. Some aren't using tampons or birth control because they're too squeamish. Given the epidemics of teen pregnancy, chlymidia, and AIDS, their lack of self-knowledge is dangerous.

And so, masturbating is also a way of de-alienating ourselves from our bodies, of literally taking our sexuality into our own hands and figuring out for ourselves Which Way is Up.

Which is a good thing. For we really can't feel comfortable sexually with other people if we don't feel comfortable with ourselves first. And if we don't know the way around our own private theme park, how is anybody else supposed to?

It we're not familiar with our own bodies and passions, every touch can leave us feeling vulnerable, threatened, or bewildered. And every lover who makes us feel good has power over us, holding a monopoly on our own pleasure. The more we're literally in touch with ourselves, the more informed and in control we are. It makes it just that much easier for us to say either yes *or* no with self-assurance. Talk about "self-help."

Besides, as Woody Allen once said, "Don't knock masturbation. It's sex with someone I love." And self-love, for women, is particularly crucial and hard won.

So why shouldn't sisters be doin' it for ourselves? My grandma used to say, "If God hadn't wanted us to touch ourselves, he would've made our arms shorter." Now there's a thought, coming from a ninety-one-year-old.

The challenge now, of course, is to find some good, female-centric slang that allows us to rap about it.

Obviously, there's "letting your fingers do the walking," "self-servicing," and "petting the kitty."

"Strumming the happy banjo" has a certain folksy appeal, though it does sound a little like having Gomer Pyle in your pants. "Visiting Disneyland" has a wholesome, family-friendly ring to it—and it would certainly give new meaning to those "I'm going to Disneyland!" commercials.

"Having a Calgon moment" has a certain *je ne sais quoi*. "Gettin' happy with yourself" is pretty much to the point, though still oblique enough to qualify as a euphemism. Ditto for "engaging in a hot-button issue."

"Surfing the Net" is well suited to our generation (and, hell, who needs a Pentium processor to operate the software?).

"Pushing your button," "taking care of yourself," and "giving lip service," all give the boys a run for their thesaurus.

My personal favorite, however, is "voting Republican."

While "voting Republican" might not strike a lot of people as being in any way synonymous with masturbation, when you consider how self-serving a lot of the party's right wing is, voting for them and jerking off really aren't that dissimilar, are they? So, that one gets my lusty, liberal vote. Next time you go to a store to purchase a vibrator, make sure you hold it up and announce as loudly as possible, "I'm gettin' ready to go vote Republican!"

That should give you a fine, cheap thrill even before you get home with the goodies.

Part II

∞

Playing Well with Others

Chapter 8

ᏇᏇ

Our Booty, Ourselves

He said he liked to do it backwards.
I said that's just fine with me—
that way we can fuck and watch TV.
—Liz Phair

Okay, is there anything that *hasn't* been said publicly about sex yet?

Well, actually, yes. Never mind that people regularly say *pussy* on HBO now, or that it's now possible to use the words *blow job* and *House subcommittee* in the same sentence. For all the titillation in the media today, our nation's understanding about women's sexuality is still about as flimsy as a thong from Victoria's Secret.

I mean, for starters: What is it with sex in the movies? First, there's not nearly enough of it. Second, how is it that screenwriters can master the intricacies of computer hacking or thermonuclear warfare, yet have no clue about foreplay? I can't tell you how many scenes I've watched in which a guy (usually thirty years older than his leading lady) hikes up a woman's skirt and brings her to orgasm in the same amount of time it takes to thaw an Eggo waffle in the microwave. Or in which a couple reaches mutual orgasm in perfect synch. Or in which the woman comes gasping demurely instead of clawing her lover's back and screaming like an auctioneer. *Hel-lo*, but do people really think this is realistic, let alone technically possible? According to Shere Hite, only one-third of us gals ever come from straight intercourse, and we certainly don't just cruise around like a well-lubed convertible all the time. We need our motors warmed up, our spark plugs sparked, and someone's head under our hood for a good long while, please, before they take us out for a ride.

Second, what's up with all the women's magazines? The way they write about sex, you'd think it was a lasso—something mostly to help us rope a guy and reel him in. "*His* G-Spot: Find It, Touch It, Watch Him Worship the Ground You Walk On," says *Cosmo*, in a typical coverline.

His G-spot? Excuse me, but last time I checked, it wasn't the *girls* who needed a road map to find their way around someone's genitals. And, frankly, why should we worry about a guy's G-spot? With only two-thirds of us capable of orgasm at all, shouldn't we be more concerned with our own little Chipwich?

Yet worst of all is the sexual sanctimony that lurks just beneath the surface. Sex is so fundamental, any primate can do it. Cole Porter wrote a song cataloging all the boinking that goes on in the animal kingdom. But let a girl have a little party in her panties and our culture goes batshit. When all the soft-core fantasies and commercialism are stripped way, Americans still tend to view women's sexual activity as slightly pathological.

Watch a little Jerry, Jenny, or Ricki, and you'll hear so many people calling sexually active women "bitches," "ho's," and "sluts," you'll think you're back in seventh grade, putting on Lipsmackers in the bathroom.

Or read the recent backlash books: *A Return to Modesty*, by Wendy Shalit; or *What Our Mothers Didn't Tell Us*, by Danielle Crittenden.

Both argue that we gals should "regain" our "power" by reviving a long-lost art: cock teasing. According to the authors, men are sexual pigs; the only *real* reason we gals roll around with them in the mud is because we've been tricked by feminists into believing that we're sexual free agents who can fuck just like guys. (This must be news to the feminists, who are usually accused of prudery.) And because we roll around with men in the mud, the books argue, men no longer respect us or want to marry us. (Which must be news to the thirty-two-billion-dollar wedding industry.) For true, lasting intimacy and love, the authors contend, women are better off demurely dangling our sexuality in front of men like a doggie biscuit until they salivate, roll over, and beg—with an engagement ring in hand, of course.

Now, c'mon: Does sexual blackmail really seem like a good recipe for true love and intimacy?

What's missing from all of this blather is an understanding about what *truly* motivates women sexually. Clearly, the world still doesn't get it. In the wake of the new millennium, our culture still assumes that women have sex for really only one of four reasons: (1) to have babies, (2) because we're "in love," (3) because we're sluts, (4) because we're only semiconscious—that is, we've been influenced by peer pressure, have low self-esteem, don't know any better. Or, oh yeah, we've been tricked by feminists into thinking we can boink like boys.

Yeah. Well. We gals have sex for all sorts of reasons that are often very nuanced, complex, or even banal. We have sex because we're horny. We have sex because we're bored. We have sex because we're passionate and insecure and curious and needy. We have sex because our hormones are so turbo-charged that we feel as if pheromones are boiling off our skin in a vapor. We have sex for noble reasons and stupid reasons.

Since I don't want to betray any of my friends' trust, I'll offer myself up as an unspectacular example. (I'll probably regret confessing to this in print, but okay): I once slept with a guy because he looked like Jon Bon Jovi, he knew how to read tarot cards, and we had almost identical record collections. Now, does this sound to you like a particularly brilliant reason to sleep with someone? Nuh-uh, not to me either. Not *now*. But when I was eighteen, it seemed like an act of genius. I'd been reading a lot of Rimbaud and I guess something about the situation struck me as daring and fantastical-ly romantic and sophisticated. I was very cavalier about it. And it made me feel great. So: Was I a victim or a vixen? Was I forfeiting my "power" or abusing it? My reasoning might have been silly, but was it "immoral"?

To assume that women sleep with people simply because we're "promiscuous" or "have low self-esteem" is as ridiculous as assum-ing that the only reason we *don't* sleep with people is because we're "responsible," "pure," or "prudish."

Casting female sexuality in simplistic, all-or-nothing terms is insulting. Not only that, it's dangerous. Certainly it skews and over-simplifies any discussion about teen pregnancy, STDs, or abstinence. It gives young women—and the world in general—a limited under-standing of who we are. It creates the illusion that something is wrong with us if we can't "just say no." And it denies that we're complicated and suffer from conflicting desires—in other words, that we're fully human.

All of this, of course, makes us less powerful. If we don't under-stand our own true sexual natures, we're less likely to make smart choices at a time when the stakes are higher, when we're already caught in our own sexual tug-of-war, pulled by mounting pressure to say yes and mounting reasons to say no.

Plus, in a culture that's essentially caught in a Celebrity Death Match between hypersexuality and puritanism, we can feel shame when we should feel ecstasy. Or, conversely, we can get lost in the jungle of our libido without any moral compass.

We can also overlook the possibility that, sometimes, sexual activity may be a symptom of a problem that needs to be dealt with. For example, if a gal picks up people at bars every night, some-one dismissing her as a "slut" obscures the fact that, hey: Girlfriend might have a drinking problem.

Moreover, if flings are considered solely a sign of promiscuity or bad judgment, they can have some dangerous societal repercus-sions. Certainly, any nonmarital sexual activity becomes questionable in a court of law. If a woman's steady lover rapes her, if she's filing for custody of her children, or if she's a lesbian, her affairs can be used by opposing attorneys to paint her as an "unreliable" or "unfit" mother or witness. In the Preppy Murder case in 1986, the victim, Jennifer Levin, had written about her fledgling affairs in her diary. The defense tried to use this against her, as proof that she was promiscuous. Nobody thought to suggest that a young woman who has affairs and writes about them in her diary is clearly a romantic. Or is obviously looking for love. Or is simply experiencing a healthy sexual curiosity at age nineteen.

So, in the name of replacing simplistic explanations with broader, more accurate possibilities, in the name of replacing stereotypes with understanding, and in the name of replacing passivity with the power of self-knowledge, we women need to talk about why we *really* have sex. I'm not talking about sharing the gooey details of our first fuck and so forth: We've been there, done that, and at this point, frankly, the world doesn't need another confession about the first time we had an orgasm on top of a pool table. Instead, we need to discuss our motivations. The world's gotta recognize that our sexuality is not simply a matter of naivete or nymphomania. We have as many motivations as there are positions in the *Kama Sutra*. So here, pooled from a vast array of women, and listed from *A* to *Z*, are just a few:

> **Affirmation.** We're good enough, we're hot enough, and, doggone it, people *want* us.

> **Anthropology.** We always wondered what it would be like to have sex with another woman/an aborigine/a white person/a quadriplegic/a Republican.

> **Appeasement.** If I have sex with you, maybe you'll: (a) quit yelling, (b) quit whining, (c) stop buggin' me about doing my taxes, (d) stop badgering me about that cutie I flirted with at the bowling alley.

> **Attention.** More people pay attention to us when we're sleeping with someone. Nobody finds it interesting if we said *no* last night—again. In fact, when has celibacy ever

been captivating in secular culture? The last so-called great novel that centered around a woman saying no was *Pamela*, which was so interminable, it was enough to make you want to become an illiterate nymphomaniac.

Babies. Duh.

Cash. Boy, what men won't do for a blow job.

Catharsis. Cheaper than therapy.

Comparison shopping. Like the song says, "You better shop around."

The Conceptual-art fuck. A lot like good real estate: Location is everything. Examples; sex on motorcycles, in glass elevator of Detroit Renaissance Center, atop grave of abusive ex-husband, while skydiving, and so on. While the sex itself may be negligible, it does make for something wild to tell our grandchildren, if we're that type of granny.

Cool toys. Wow, this person has a Humvee and a waterbed. Wow, this person has an airplane. Wow, this person has a bottle of Reddi-wip. A strap-on dildo. Three-dozen peacock feathers and a vanilla-flavored dental dam. Whatever.

Depression. Hey, it's cheaper than therapy or Prozac.

Diet sex. Hey, it's either fuck or eat. Which burns more calories?

The Don't-leave-me/please-call-me-again fuck. Don't ask us why, but we still think this actually works.

Drunkenness. Often includes wicked hangover, in more ways than one.

The Easier-to-say-yes-than-no fuck. Can be close to date rape, though more the result of apathy, fatigue, or boredom than submission.

Escape. Sex because it gets us out of our head, distracts us from our pain, neurosis, or fear. Sort of like physical equivalent of television or, for outdoorsy types, mountain biking.

Excitement. Better than ride at a theme park; usually includes emotional roller coaster.

Fantasy. They read Pablo Neruda's love poetry aloud and feed us bananas Foster. The sun is setting outside the cabana. There is Dom Pérignon, bubble bath, and Bocelli on the box. "Come to me," they say, in a languid, smoky voice. What girl could resist? It's just like in those Harlequin books we keep reading.

Fear. We worry that they'll get angry, act crazy, or say something bad about us if we say no.

To Feel "adult." What else can we do if we're not old enough to drink beer and we already smoke and drive?

To Feel alive, sexy, and young. Like, du-uh.

To Feel desired. Duh again.

To Feel powerful. Triple duh.

Glamour. Sex with rock star, actor, billionaire, cool leftie activist, tortured poet, athlete, local bigwig, and so on.

To Get a clue. Usually sex for beginners or between new partners. Often like biology class or, in some cases, shop class.

To Get presents. What some of us won't do for jewelry. Or maybe a Happy Meal.

Great for our looks. Provides better glow than Clinique.

Guilt. He/she bought us dinner, helped us change our flat tire, came to our emotional rescue, fed our dog: We owe them.

The Hire-me fuck. Just when we thought it was finally safe to go back in the water, it seems the casting couch lives on. Also close to date rape, though force involved is usually economic/professional.

The I'm-on-a-vacation-in-a-foreign-country fuck. Otherwise known as the "hey-what-the-fuck" fuck. Fun, though usually terrible PR for American women abroad.

To Incite jealousy. Yoohoo! Over here! Look what I'm doing! Eat your heart out!

Intimacy. Because playing Pictionary and drinking latté only goes so far.

Loneliness. Not to be underestimated. Often more powerful aphrodisiac than lust.

Love. Ditto.

Make-up sex. A better, faster peace accord.

To Make people like us. Don't ask us why, but we still think this works, too.

To Manipulate. *You wannit? You wannit? You wannit? Say please . . .*

The Melodrama fuck. We sleep with our lover's best friend, someone married, or the person our best friend has a crush on—anything to really make everyone's life miserable—because we get some sort of sick pleasure out of the attention and drama. In other words, we make a mess *because we can.*

The Mercyfuck. We basically think that having sex with this person entitles us to a tax deduction for making a charitable donation. We don't get off from the sex so much as from the idea that our lover is so helpless/inexperienced/needy/in lust with us, he or she will be eternally grateful to us for sleeping with them.

Natural high. Fabulous source of endorphins—without having to wear sweat pants, listen to aerobics instructor, buy running shoes.

Nostalgia. This could be with our ex, or someone who reminds us of our ex, or someone who reminds us of an earlier time in our life, or someone we once had a crush on and now that we actually have the opportunity to sleep with them, we feel like we can't turn them down, if only because our younger self would've killed for it.

Nothing on television. Six hundred cable stations, and for what?

Peer pressure. We know: *If all of our friends jumped off the Empire State Building, would we?* Well, what if jumping off the Empire State Building increased our social status and maybe gave us an orgasm?

This Person-is-so-hot-I-have-to-sleep-with-them-immediately-or-I-will-die. Self-explanatory.

To Please someone else. Hey, some of us just refuse to cook or clean.

Poor-excuse-for-a-hug fuck. What we really want is to be held, but the person won't come home with us unless we sleep with them.

The Post-mortem fuck. Not to be confused with necrophilia. Impulse after a funeral, witnessing of an accident, death of a loved one.

The Powerfuck. Not a reason we like to admit to. Generally entails sleeping with someone because we get off on the control we have over them, such as when they're younger than us, our underling at work, our student, or our blackmail-able boss.

The Prove-something fuck. "See, I'm not gay. I'm sleeping with men." "See, I'm desirable." "See, I can get someone cute, so people will respect me."

The Rebound fuck. Combination of healing and distraction after heartbreak. To escape from the grief, to prove we're still desirable, and usually done with secret hope that our ex will hear about it. Consequently, we don't kiss-and-tell—we kiss-and-broadcast. Like over the Internet.

Revenge. Sort of like what Lorena Bobbit did, only psychological. Motives differ, too: "You've cheated on me? Fine. I'll get even." "That will show you never to forget my birthday again." "She took my lover, so I'll take hers."

Self-education. Nothing like getting a little experience under our belt.

Sport. Contest with roommate, best friend, even self. Centers around challenge, pursuit, acquisition, quantity. Often high risk of STDs, emotional chaos. Not something we generally want to admit to, either.

The That'll-show-my-parents fuck. A Freudian field day: "Boy, Daddy would fall off his polo pony if he caught me here with his Jamaican stable boy." "That's it, baby. Give it to me right here on her plastic slipcovers." "Of course my mom doesn't mind. I always sleep with her boyfriends."

The Wait'll-I-tell-my-friends fuck. A biggie for writers, braggarts, anyone with sense of self-invention.

Whoops—watching the porno channel again.

Whoops—vibrator out of batteries.

And last, but certainly not least, the number-one reason why women have sex:

Because it's fun and it feels good.

And let's not let the world forget it.

Chapter 9

☙❧

Every Idiot We Date Is One
Less Idiot We Risk Marrying

When I'm dating, I look at a guy and
wonder, "Is this the man I want my
children to spend their weekends with?"
—RITA RUDNER

Okay, let's face it: Dating sucks. There are no two ways about it. Let's not let the comic books, movies, or magazines tell us otherwise. Dating is a misery. Gay or straight, male or female, everybody hates it.

Dating is a job audition, beauty contest, and public-speaking engagement all in one. Except if it's a blind date. Then it has the assault of a surprise party thrown in, too. Of course, somebody's already tipped us off about the surprise part ahead of time. We still don't know what to expect—only that we'll be visually ambushed and compelled to feign enjoyment.

And the person we're being fixed up with feels exactly the same way.

And we both know it.

Ugh.

There are always a few annoying people who say things like, "But I really *like* dating. It's *fun* to go out and meet new people." Yeah, well. Either these people are selling pyramid schemes or they fuck everybody they hook up with and that suits 'em just fine. But most people hate dating so much, we consider getting married just to avoid it.

Now, as far as we gals are concerned, we know that there is nothing inherently empowering about dating for us. But, then again, there is nothing inherently empowering about dating for anybody. In this way, ironically, dating may be a great equalizer: After all, it reduces all of us to self-conscious, preening Bundles of Need. It's not like, say, art class, childbirth, or kick boxing, where some of us clearly have an edge over others.

Of course, one could argue that dating is slightly riskier for women because more of us tend to be abused and killed by people we're romantically involved with. To put it mildly: This is not good news. But then, what the hell are we supposed to do? Sit home with our cats for the next eighty years watching public television? (Not that there's anything wrong with that.)

Obviously, there are some ways we gals must try and protect ourselves. I mean, like, duh: Don't give our phone number to some schmuck in a bar just because we're afraid of "hurting his feelings." Meet in public. Stay relatively sober. Try to keep the libido in check. And, whenever possible, pay our own way.

Yeah, I know this last bit of advice is going to piss off a few people, but c'mon, let's not kid ourselves: Money is power. There are still too many guys out there who think that if they treat us to something, we *owe* them or they *own* us. So I say: Let's not go there. Our autonomy is worth at least a fifteen-dollar dinner. Besides, there are often so many unknowns and miscommunications when we first start dating, why compound the confusion with money issues? If we really like a guy, it's nice to make it clear that we see him as more than a meal ticket. Plus, if guys don't have their wallets to rely on, they may actually have to develop things like listening skills and better personalities. This, too, is worth at least a fifteen-dollar dinner.

Beyond that, I believe we must avoid at all cost men who subscribe to *Soldier of Fortune* magazine, crackheads, fundamentalist Baptist yahoos, men who refuse to take their lithium, Sensitive New Age Guys who are so busy bragging about how enlightened and feminist they are that we can't get a word in edgewise, any guy who uses bronzing gel, Amway salesmen, alcoholics, and anyone over twenty-one who's still playing with his Game Boy.

Otherwise, if we want to find romance, we single sisters have to keep taking risks and go out on dates. Why? Because, whether we're gay or straight, if we want to be with someone, we gotta kick some game. Short of an arranged marriage, it's the only way to get from *A* to *B*. And, face it, there's only one thing worse than picking at a Southwest Fiesta platter at TGIF's while someone we barely know rehashes old Jeff Foxworthy jokes over the blare of the jukebox. And that is: sitting at home watching "Pop-up Video" and wishing we were out with someone.

So, how might we survive the real-life versions of the Dating Game, Love Connection, and Singled Out without sacrificing our sanity or self-esteem?

1. **Abandon all hope.** More than anything else, my fellow femmes, I think it's crucial that we change our attitude. Stop thinking positively. Kiss expectation good-bye. Say *adios* to optimism.

   Why?

   Because we shouldn't be masochists.

   And dating is a process of elimination.

   Dating isn't simply about meeting someone. It's a screening process. It's like the Brita filter for romance. I mean, how else are we going to figure out whom we want to be with and what we're *really* looking for, except through trial, error, and experience?

   The things we value in someone when we're fifteen—say, their ability to look really cool playing air guitar—are not what we want when we're twenty-two (a photographer who can get us into nightclubs for free)—which is not, in turn, what we want when we're thirty (a guy as solid as his credit rating). And this maturation comes from dating enough players, pseudo–rock stars, and pretentious intellectuals to realize that their appeal actually has its limits.

Bad dates are inevitable, but they are a crucial, necessary education. As my friend Desa likes to say, "Every bad date brings you closer to Joe." Joe is Desa's kind, handsome, doting, and impossibly suave husband. Joe is amazing with a capital *A*. Joe is the bomb with a capital *B*. Joe is a catch with a capital *C*. Pick your letter: The guy's the whole damn alphabet. But lemme tell you, that's almost what Desa had to go through herself before she met Joe. Just as she watched me date some guy who collected lizards and another who got called in for police lineups on a regular basis, I watched her date a guy whose life's ambition seemed to be packing groceries and another whose primary pastime seemed to be falling off his skateboard and flirting with her mother.

But with each guy, Desa learned something. And she learned enough that by the time she met Joe, she was smart enough to appreciate him and know that he had what she wanted.

Hence, her motto. And mine, which is a variation of hers: Every idiot we go out with is one less idiot we risk spending our lives with.

Knowing this, it's counterproductive to build up our expectations. Because we're all tempted to treat each new date as our own personal Academy Awards. We run out to buy a new outfit for the occasion. We hope, imagine, and pray that this evening will be *it*—that we'll finally be chosen—and that we'll wind up hurrying down the aisle and delivering our acceptance speech. But if it doesn't happen, we feel devastated. Dear Goddess, why put ourselves through that?

Better to get dressed, singing, "Another One Bites the Dust." That way, if the evening does not turn out to be a total disaster, we'll be pleasantly surprised.

2. **It's not a date. It's entertainment.** The real purpose of a date is not to meet someone. The real purpose of a date is so that we can tell our gal-pals about it the next day.

    Since ninety-nine percent of all dates we'll ever be on will end in disappointment, we're far better off approaching each date as a source of endless entertainment and mockery for ourselves and our friends.

    This way, when the guy our aunt Myrna fixed us up with drools and picks his teeth with his salad fork, so what?

    So what if the woman we met at Ani DiFranco spent the whole evening stalking her ex-girlfriend?

    So what if the guy who asked us out at the health club arrived at the restaurant with a tape measure and a checklist? The fact that we emptied a bowl of lobster bisque into his lap and called him a fascist only enhances our story for posterity.

    Nothing takes the sting our of any truly bad date like detachment and humor. Goddess knows these are often the first things to get lost in all the clouds of expectation and antiperspirant beforehand.

3. **We feel your pain.** Besides, little else makes women feel as empowered as shared humiliation and misery. (Why do you think we watch all those talk shows?)

    Especially when it comes to dating. Sure, we're occasionally heartened by stories of women who give up trying to meet someone, then meet their One True Love at the Laundromat.

    But when we've just arrived home from an evening where our date spent the whole time making racist jokes and touching his crotch, we really don't want to hear about other people's happiness. We derive far more comfort listening to a friend of ours who just went on a date with someone who got lost on the way to her house, arrived three hours late, and then had the *cajones* to hit her up for gas money.

    We're far more comforted by hearing that our girl Inez went out with someone who got so drunk playing beer-pong with his old frat buddies, he had to get his stomach pumped.

Or that Barbara got set up with someone who turned out to be her demented third cousin—the one who's twenty-three and still busy with his Pokémon collection.

We've all gone out with some hottie, hoping that maybe this person will finally be The One, only to arrive home feeling disappointed, or rejected, or duped. We discover that a person whom we fantasized about actually doesn't believe in teaching evolution. Or is recovering from electroshock therapy. Or is thirty-eight and still living with his parents. Or that it's his life's ambition to move to Minnesota and run for political office. Or that she has "sexuality issues."

Somebody who tells us that she went on one date and "just knew this was the person I'd spend the rest of my life with" is an idiot. Sure, it may have happened to her, but how does this help *us*, thank you?

Next time you have a shitty date—or suspect that you will—remember that you're going on it not for yourself but for the good of all womankind. Your misery is our comfort.

4. **Fuck decorum and false advertising.** So many of us—especially straight gals—are taught to be "a lady," and to act "like a creature unlike any other" on a date. And because of this, we put up with far more crap than we ought to.

We say yes to a second date because we don't want to "be mean"—even if the guy is about as interesting as a dial tone and his most redeeming quality is that he can breathe unassisted by a respirator.

We get into our date's Jeep Cherokee—even though he's just had fourteen Jell-O shots—because we don't want to "offend him."

We misrepresent our needs and desires in the hope that it will make us more likeable. *Oh, that's okay,* we say, *I don't mind that you went ahead and ordered for me; really, I love fried clams and cheese fries. And, yeah, I'm a huge Raiders fan, too.*

Hey, there are manners, and then there is false advertising.

Lead him to think we like football and chances are we'll

wind up sitting through the whole fucking season with some-body who's painted his chest black and silver with grease paint.

If we don't tell a guy we're not interested in him, because we don't want to "hurt his feelings," how is he supposed to know to get lost? Instead, we'll just let him call and call, until he's angry and feels like an asshole—while we complain to our friends that he's bugging us. (I mean, if we think saying no is going to hurt a guy's feelings, imagine what a restraining order will do.)

So let's be honest. Not brutally honest. Just clear. It's a mat-ter of treating both ourselves and our dates with respect.

Case in point: About seven years ago, I met this really cute guy at a bar. I'll call him "Sam" because that's what his name was. We stayed up all night talking, dancing, smooching. As much as anyone can tell from a single chance encounter assisted by a couple of frozen margaritas (okay, four), Sam and I were amazing together. At the end of the date, he gave me his num-ber (I was in the process of moving) and urged me to call once I had a phone. Yet when I telephoned a week later, he sounded decidedly less enthused.

"Look," he told me, "this is awkward, especially since I only had one date with you. But since I met you, my ex-girlfriend has come back into my life. I'm not sure what's going to hap-pen, but I don't feel comfortable starting something with you right now. I thought about just not telling you, or stringing you along, or blowing you off. But I don't want to do that. I like you, and I don't want to treat you disrespectfully."

Zowie. Now let me tell you, Girlfriends. When he told me that he didn't want to see me, for a moment I felt a quick little stab to the heart. But then I felt relief and gratitude—because at least I knew where I stood and was allowed to keep my dig-nity. Had his ex-girlfriend really come back into his life? Who the hell knows. But he said no clearly and respectfully, in a way that didn't make me feel personally diminished.

The fact that I still remember this little encounter is a sign of how rare such behavior is—and how much I appreciated it.

There was no bitterness on my part, or any feelings of self-blame, self-doubt, or self-flagellation. Since then I've tried to treat the guys I've said no to the same way. It ain't easy, but it's less stressful—and certainly less costly than Caller ID.

5. An ounce of closure is worth a pound of pride. It's generally assumed that if someone is blowing us off, the best course of action is to accept it and move on. If a guy says he's going to call and then two weeks go by, write him off. Don't call him. Don't give him the satisfaction of hearing your neediness, desire, and disappointment. Just walk away, Renee. Hold your head high. Don't cry out loud. "Rules girls" know when to walk. *Blah blah blah . . .*

Yeah, well: You know how many friends I have who are actually capable of such self-restraint and discipline?

Exactly one.

My friend Gwynne, Goddess bless her, can actually say: *Fuck him. That's it. If that bastard thinks I'm going to call him, he can die a long cold death in hell.*

The rest of us snivelers? We enter what my friend Bari calls The Demented Zone.

We may know in our hearts that it's over, but damned if our heads don't keep stoking the eternal flame of hope. No excuse is too implausible, no loophole too small. Our thinking gets so creative, we could be awarded a grant from the NEA for conceptual art: *Well, maybe he was sent to Kenya on business and he went on a safari and a puma ate his cell phone,* we say. *Maybe there was a death in his family and he's too convulsed with grief to move his jaw or his index finger. Maybe his car overturned on the way to the dentist's and he's been lying in a ditch for three days with a fractured neck.*

Whatever it is, we will come up with a seemingly valid reason to justify calling him. And ninety-nine percent of the time, whenever we do finally reach the guy, we hear what we suspected all along: the temperature at the other end of the line plunging into the single digits. A lot of hemming and hawing. Poor excuses from a poor excuse. And then we feel like idiots.

I never should have called, we say. *I should have preserved my pride.*

Yeah, well: Fuck pride. We can all live without pride for a day. But *closure*? There's a reason that families whose loved ones were declared missing in action in Vietnam thirty years ago are still lobbying Congress to find the bodies. On some level, we humans cannot let go of someone until we actually see the corpse.

The same holds true for dating. If we've invested even an iota of hope in someone, we often have to confirm that the hookup has been permanently disconnected—that the promise is completely dead and buried—before we can move on. And if this means demeaning ourselves a little, and calling when we shouldn't, and telling the guy that he's behaved like an asshole, and flogging the thing to death, so be it. A little short-term humiliation can be empowering in the long run.

After all, in the end it just brings us closer to Joe.

Chapter 10

ഐ

Fish Who Need Bicycles
(A Thinking Girl's
Guide to Love)

---

*Cinderella lied to us. There should be
a Betty Ford Center where they
de-program you by putting you in an
electric chair, play "Some Day My
Prince Will Come," and hit you and go
"Nobody's coming . . . Nobody's coming
. . . Nobody's coming."*

—JUDY CARTER

Ah, a rare harmonic convergence has occurred! Every single one of my girlfriends has fallen in love with someone! Every single gal-pal of mine is in the throes of a True Romance! Which means of course that, as of now, we are all clinically insane.

We're not getting valentines every day but heart palpitations. We're not breathless but hyperventilating. With panic. And expectation. And the unsettling feeling that what we've dreamed about and what we're actually living are two completely alternative universes.

Because besides diets and relatives, nothing really causes us gals more angst than love—romantic love, with the O shaped like a heart and a lot of insipid bluebirds flying around it. Never mind that intimacy in all forms can feel as treacherous as it can feel exhilarating. From the time we're old enough to sit in a high chair, girls are spoon-fed a slew of sadistic little fairy tales about romance, all supposedly in the name of "entertainment."

Along with our strained carrots, we're given tales to swallow about women who were comatose until men rescued them. About women who were consigned to spend their lives dust-busting for their evil stepmothers until men rescued them. About women who were locked in towers until their hair grew long enough for men to shimmy up like a flagpole in order to rescue them. About women who traded their voice for a fabulous pair of legs so that men would love them (now what's the message in *that*?). About women whose beauty was so great, they transformed men's hearts and minds faster than a near-death experience on the Santa Monica Freeway or a midlife crisis.

Yep, a few years in a playpen with Walt Disney and the Brothers Grimm and, as far as I'm concerned, we sisters are finished in the romance department. From then on, ninety-nine percent of what we hear and believe about love is just plain wrong. Pabulum. Horsepucky. Cockamamie. Whackness. Merde. Choose your vernacular—anyway you slice it, it comes out peanuts.

As we get older, it gets no better. Between talk shows, romance novels, movies, soap operas, and magazines, more misleading information is imparted to women about love than about cigarettes.

Compounding this, of course, are the messages we get telling us that powerful women don't need romance, that strong women are unlovable, and that single women over the age of thirty-five have a better chance of getting hit by a stray torpedo than of landing a husband.

Sweet Venus, love is difficult enough without all the false advertising! How can enlightened and powerful goddesses sort through the mixed messages and emerge truly ready for romance? I say, for starters, let's pull the wings off some fairy tales.

FAIRY TALE NUMBER 1.

ⓖⓢ

If you're a strong woman, everyone will think you're a man-hating lesbian and no one will love you.

Oh *pul-leze.* That is, like, so twenty minutes ago. As if Oprah, Madonna, Courtney Love, Whoopi Goldberg, Sandra Day O'Connor, Margaret Thatcher, Roseanne, Ruth Bader Ginsburg, Aretha Franklin, Cher, Candice Bergen, and Diane Sawyer, to name a few, have never been loved?

Besides, it's not the lesbians who are usually the big man-haters. The most vitriol I've heard spewed against people with XY chromosomes has actually come from us straight chicks. We're far more likely to be disappointed, hurt, and enraged by men than lesbians are. After all, what does a dyke care if some guy belches during a moment of silence at a funeral? She doesn't have to cuddle with him afterward in the parking lot. For dykes, men are sort of like watching elephants fart at the zoo: The guys are funny and disgusting, and then, after the entertainment is over, the lesbians can go home and leave the mess behind. It's us straight girls who are stuck there in the cage as the cleanup crew.

FAIRY TALE NUMBER 2.

ⓖⓢ

If you're a strong woman, you don't need a lover.

Yeah, yeah. We've all heard the saying: "A woman without a man is like a fish without a bicycle." Well, some of us fishes want a brand-new red Schwinn with hybrid tires and a gel seat—and it doesn't mean we're misguided or weak. Gay or straight, male or female, some of us just long for romantic companionship. Ain't no shame in that. Life is hard and lonely; it's only natural to want someone to share the misery with.

FAIRY TALE NUMBER 3.

ᘒᘒ

All single women are miserable.

An article appeared in the *Washington Post* once around Valentine's Day with the headline, "One Is the Loveliest Number: Two Single Washington Women, Singularly Happy." Apparently, the fact that women can actually be happy by ourselves is *news*! I mean, stop the presses! Had the reporter really done his homework, however, I suspect that he could've found more than two women. Why, there may even be five or six.

My friend Karen, who's solo by choice, says, "Every time I'm in a relationship, I feel like I'm a car with the air conditioning on all the time. Sure, I can go, but my engine just can't run as well." Studies show that there are more single women in America than ever before—and that more of us are single by choice—and that we're thriving. So if we're flying solo, we have plenty of company. Not having a mate doesn't mean we have "nothing." It may mean we have standards, though. And, oh yeah, a life.

FAIRY TALE NUMBER 4.

ᘒᘒ

The cheese stands alone.

Speaking of sadistic things from childhood, remember the game the Farmer in the Dell? All the kids get in a circle and dance around while the farmer picks a wife, the wife picks a child, the child picks a cow, the cow picks a dog, and so forth, until nobody's left unpicked except for the cheese, who stands alone in the middle of the circle while everyone dances around "it," squealing, "The cheese stands alone! The cheese stands alone!"

For most of us, this is our mortal fear—that we will be the cheese. We get the idea that if we do not find a partner by, say, age thirty-five, we will stand alone and be mocked by everyone around us for the rest of eternity.

Well, it doesn't work out that way. Love blossoms for all different people at all different ages. Our culture won't tell us this, of course, because it wants to sell us lots of stuff like Retin-A anti-aging cream and liposuction. But my mother works at an old-age home, so she can attest to the fact that there are octogenarians running around goo-goo–eyed over each other. *People* magazine is another source of proof: The folks profiled in its glossy pages have inevitably met their loves at all different stages of their lives, in all different capacities.

Besides, as the French know, cheese gets better and more desirable with age. Better to be a fine wheel of brie than just another slab o' Velveeta.

FAIRY TALE NUMBER 5.

❧

Prince Charmings want beautiful, young princesses.

Not according to the *real* fairy tales of the twentieth century. When Edward VIII, future king of England, abdicated the throne, it was for Wallis Simpson, an older divorcée. And although Princess Diana was young, gorgeous, and well-dressed, Prince Charles ultimately left her for a woman his own age with unspectacular looks.

Sure, there are always doofuses who want trophy wives, or Peter Pans who like women thirty years younger than them. But that's not the whole picture.

A lot of guys, when it comes right down to it, just want a woman they can fart in front of. Yeah, they wouldn't mind if we were cute, too, but the real bottom line is that they want someone they can be comfortable with, whom they can wake up beside feeling peaceful, whom they can talk to and laugh with. They may say they want Rebecca Romijn-Stamos, but if we sleep with them, let them "control" the remote, and don't cause them any pain, they can be ecstatic and grateful.

They're like us in that way. If they're grown-ups—and granted, that can be a big *if*—what guys really want in a lover is a best friend, albeit with boobs.

FAIRY TALE NUMBER 6.

෨෨

True love is instant. We'll know it the minute we see the person.

Pudding is instant. Real love and intimacy take time. This is a pretty hard concept to grasp for all of us who've been raised watching *Love Boat* reruns and flirting on the Internet, but a healthy relationship does require more than sharing piña coladas on the Lido Deck or sending each other, ahem, hotmail. Trust, communication, and kindness—which we can't always gauge on the first date, much less the fourth—take time to unveil and build.

Besides, think about what made for an "instant" connection when we were fifteen: The fact that the guy looked like Lenny Kravitz, we smoked pot together listening to "Free Bird," and agreed that everybody else in our school was a jerk.

Fairy Tale Number 7.

❧

Boys tease us because they like us.

No, boys tease us because they're assholes. Abuse is not an acceptable expression of love. If a guy mistreats us, it's not his own little quirky way of expressing love—it's an exercise of possessiveness, control, and ego. We gotta run, do not walk, to the nearest exit.

"Bad boys" may be sexy during our rebellious years in high school, but we should outgrow them as quickly as a Ricky Martin lunchbox. We gotta put a stop to that "Beauty and the Beast" mentality where girls are taught that our love and devotion alone can transform a monster into a prince. A relationship is not a reformatory.

Besides, we gals are not a 7-Eleven: always open, always convenient, always there to serve and assist, with no needs of our own.

Fairy Tale Number 8.

❧

If we don't have a date for Valentines Day, we're unworthy and pathetic.

The truth is, ninety-nine percent of the population is miserable on Valentine's Day. Hell, the holiday commemorates a massacre. Shouldn't that tell us something? Come February 14, the singles feel wretched and excluded, and the couples feel under enormous pressure to live up to some fatuous romantic fantasy cooked up by Hallmark: Show me the flowers. Cough up the jewelry. Load me up on Prozac and take me out to dinner. Every relationship is thrown into a kiln for twenty-four hours, where it's forced to withstand pressure and heat.

Personally, I think we should revert the holiday back to its pagan roots. Long before the Catholic Church turned it into a tribute to a beheaded Christian, Valentine's Day was apparently a pagan fertility rite, sort of like a racy version of spin-the-bottle. In the fourth century B.C., young men drew the names of eligible young women randomly from a box. Whomever they picked became their companion for "mutual entertainment and pleasure" until the next year's lottery.

While I'm not suggesting that we raffle off single women to adolescent boys—or anybody to anybody—surely some sort of *inclusive* chocolate bacchanalia has got to be better than the current incarnation of the holiday. Because, first of all, who besides sixteen-year-old prom queens really has fun on Valentine's Day? And, second of all, do lovers really need a holiday? When you're in love, every day is potentially February 14. I say we let Valentine's Day be a day when the *lovelorn* get their share of the goodies and attention, when we celebrate with the celibate, dine with the divorced, and send sweets to the soloists *and* the starry-eyed alike. Make it a day when *everyone* gets to feel loved! But until this happens, I say we should all just eat a couple of heart-shaped chocolates and go to bed early.

FAIRY TALE NUMBER 9.

Lesbians have it easier.

In certain circles (particularly on college campuses), it's taken as informal gospel that lesbians have better relationships than straight couples because there's no power imbalance or oppressive gender roles involved. As if most lesbians don't have to fight for their relationships every step of the way. As if they don't have to love covertly or risk losing their jobs, being disowned, and getting beaten up by gangs of Neanderthal teenagers. As if they aren't made into political scapegoats by every hate-monger from here to Capitol Hill. As if love doesn't turn *everybody* into a vulnerable, dithering moron.

FAIRY TALE NUMBER 10.

Straights have it easier.

In certain circles, it's taken as informal gospel that heterosexual couples have it easier than lesbians because straights can show their love overtly, have ostentatious weddings, and have the entire culture aggressively reaffirm their commitment. Yeah, well, the reason that the entire culture aggressively reaffirms straight commitments is because they *have* to. Men and women often don't really understand each other, trust each other, or even like each other. Unless enormous amounts of pressure are exerted on us, chances are we might remain just the way we were in sixth grade—boys on one side of the room, girls on the other—with maybe an occasional foray into the supply room for "Three Minutes in the Closet." Besides, love turns *everybody* into a vulnerable, dithering moron.

FAIRY TALE NUMBER 11.

Bisexuals have it easier.

As Woody Allen said, "If you're bisexual, you have twice as many chances of getting a date." True, but nobody trusts you, either. Besides, love turns *everybody* into a vulnerable, dithering moron.

Fairy Tale Number 12.

ଜ୬

Love is pure bliss.

Yeah, and when you pull this leg, it plays "Jingle Bells." Like my grandma said: Love is anarchy. It turns *everybody* into a vulnerable, dithering moron.

You know what's the first thing Cinderella really did after the prince whisked her away to the castle to live happily ever after? She had a massive anxiety attack, called her therapist about "intimacy issues," and downed two bottles of Xanax.

Now that this has been cleared up, let's go forth and love with abandon!

Chapter 11

ෙ෧

Marriage Ain't Prozac

Right now, there are two things
in my life that need to be done:
me and my laundry. I want to marry
a man who can do both.

—OPHIRA EDUT

When I was five years old, the one thing I wanted to be more than anything else was a Bride. A girlie-girl of the First Order, I thought brides were the bomb. And since I had an inordinate amount of free time on my hands, I spent a lot of it walking around the house in my mother's white-chiffon nightgown with a doily on my head.

Needless to say, this thrilled my relatives.

"Oh, look! Susie's getting *married!*" they'd coo approvingly. "Who's the groom?"

Groom? What groom?

As far as I was concerned, "bride" was about being fabulous and adored. "Bride" was about having a tiara. "Bride" was about being the center of attention. What did any of this have to do with a *groom?*

But the adults said, "Surely, you can't be a bride if you don't have a groom."

And there you have it.

By age five I had absorbed basically everything that drives ninety-nine percent of all women crazy for the rest of our lives. Little else makes us gals quite so anxious as the issue of "marriage." Whether we're gay or straight, puritan or progressive, we've learned by osmosis that society still considers marriage to be the center-piece of our lives, the defining achievement for a girl. Between our relatives and *The Rules*, we're under a lot of pressure. Only brides live happily ever after, we're taught: A husband holds the key to our happiness.

In the words of my five-year-old self: *Barf.*

Don't get me wrong. I'm not knocking marriage—for either straight or gay gals. In the early days of the women's movement, some feminists claimed that straight women didn't need men, that we were better off without them. Well, I don't buy *that* fairy tale, either. Let me be the first to admit that I'm not one of those lucky autonomous women whose idea of bliss is to go to the movies alone with nobody buggin' them. I've usually been fucking miser-able when I've been single. And I'm still walking around with that lace doily on my head. Well, metaphorically, anyways.

But as a progressive prima donna, I certainly don't buy that "every Princess needs a Prince" scenario, either. I mean, hel-lo. This is the twenty-first century. If I decide to ride off into the sunset all by myself, that's just as legit, thank you very much. Ditto for if I decide to ride off with another princess.

Plus, as a member of a generation whose parents divorced in record numbers, I also know that real marriage is *real* complicated. Those "drive-thru" wedding chapels in Las Vegas are insane. They perpetuate the myth that marriage is a Happy Meal—a quick, easy source of gratification and presents. Excuse me, but a good mar-riage requires serious effort. The least you can do is get out of your car.

Any honest married person will admit this: Marriage can be joyous, but it's also an out-and-out wrestling match between Romance and Disappointment, Expectation and Compromise. Tellingly, when Ann Landers was once asked what problems plague Americans the most, she replied, "The poor want to be rich, the rich want to be happy, the single want to be married, and the married want to be dead."

That should tell us something right there.

The good news, of course, is that American women today are among the first women in history who don't absolutely have to marry for protection, survival, and acceptance. We have the unprecedented luxury of choice: whether to marry, whom to marry, when to marry, and how to marry. We have power and options—and marriage itself has been legally transformed from the glorified master-and-servant relationship of the past into a more equal partnership.

All of this should be a fabulous thing for females! We finally have some control over our own emotional, sexual, spiritual, and financial destiny! The ability to make smart decisions, to make sure we're well suited to our match! Yippee! Uncork that bubbly. Throw that rice in the air. Tell that polka band from Astoria, Queens, to start playing "Respect."

Unfortunately, however, we gals are so imbued with fantasies about marriage that, too often, we approach wedlock in a state of desperation or delusion.

If we're gay, of course, marriage has been cordoned off with razor wire by sanctimonious morons—so that if we do find somebody we want to live with and care for until death do us part, things are complicated right from the start. The best that lesbians can hope for right now is to cobble together a "domestic partnership" through various legal loopholes, inclusive policies, and progressive places of worship. It's sort of *wedlite* instead of *wedlock*. Better than nothing, I suppose, but still not great for the old blood pressure.

Yet if we're straight, deciding to marry is not exactly a three-tiered cakewalk either.

Thanks to our culture, many of us view marriage through a mindset of scarcity. We're told that if we don't "hurry up" and "find" a husband, all the "good ones" will be "taken." So our search for a partner becomes like hunting for a Prada blouse during a one-day sale at Neiman-Marcus. We race to the store, tear through the racks like a maniac looking for something that "fits," and hope that we'll beat the other shoppers to the best bargain before closing time. The fact that we have to choose one outfit to wear every single day for the rest of our lives just makes us even more insane.

Others of us are so convinced we have to be married that we effectually subject ourselves to a shotgun wedding—except that we're the ones holding the pistol, and often we're holding it to our own head, if not to our boyfriend's. We *will* a marriage to occur just so we can be capital-*M* married.

Still others of us are so blinded by fantasy, so ga-ga over engagement rings and white dresses, that we really can't see past the veil over our heads. We walk down that aisle with great expectations but absolutely no clue.

Most people will agree that the decision to say "I do" should not be made lightly. And yet there is so much pressure on women to say yes automatically—to say yes for the wrong reasons—and to say yes unequivocally. We're rarely encouraged to think rationally about marriage: It's considered antiromantic. It suggests we're somehow lacking real passion and love. Nor are we encouraged to entertain much doubt—or to accept that, *Hey, all aspects of life are uncertain. Get used to it.*

In how many fairy tales does the princess tell the prince that she needs some "time to think"? That she's not sure she's "really ready"? That she "wants to work out certain issues" before she commits to spending the rest of her life in his castle?

Ideally we gals should commit to someone out of strength and desire—not fantasy or fear. This is difficult, I know. Like I said, I've walked around with that doily on my head. For that matter, I've also gone to sleep alone and teary-eyed, convinced I would never find someone as I listened to the clock tick. And when I finally did meet my Monsieur Right, people put so much pressure on me to get engaged right away, it's a wonder I didn't start producing oil.

But why relinquish our power? As my grandmother used to say, "Any two idiots can get married. And they usually do."

It's marrying well—or deciding not to—that takes real savvy. So let's forget the poofy dresses and glass slippers for a moment, and try these words of wisdom on for size instead.

1. **Holy matrimony is not the holy grail.** Certainly if it does resemble the holy grail, it's closer to the Monty Python movie. After the quest for a life partner is over, life itself continues. And this life has the potential to be just as tumultuous, frustrating, and ridiculous as singlehood.

   Marriage won't transform a cleaning lady into a princess or a beast into a prince. "A lot of people think that once they're married, their spouses will change dramatically and all the problems in their relationship will disappear," a marriage counselor told me. "That's just not true. Any problems you have before the wedding will still be there after the honeymoon."

   In fact, if "Cinderella" was written to reflect the real deal, her story might go something like this:

   > After P.C. [Prince Charming] and Cindy got back from their honeymoon, they had an idyllic month at the castle until Cindy's mother in-law, the queen, announced she was moving in. When Cindy told P.C. that either his mother was leaving or she was, P.C. said that *she* was one to talk, seeing as *her* own stepmother was quite a piece of work. Besides, he yelled, "You were nothing but a cleaning lady before you met me!"
   >
   > After babies, diapers, and years of petty arguments, Cindy had a brief fling with a pharmacist whom she met over the Internet, then got addicted to Percocet. P.C. lost a chunk of money in a Ponzi scheme and survived an unspectacular midlife crises than included an Alfa Romeo and a bulimic Brazilian debutante. In their

later years, the couple discovered in-line skating and Viagra. After Cindy had her hip replaced, they retired to Boca, where they spent the rest of their days hitting the early-bird specials, playing mah-jongg, and driving with their left blinker on.

2. **A wedding isn't a marriage.** At age five, I perceived marriage as a dress, a party, and a spotlight. Unfortunately, there's a whole industry dedicated to perpetuating this idea for females until we're, oh, fifty.

   An entire bridal industry is dedicated to feeding and exploiting our childhood dreams, to helping us obsess about stuff like a dress that makes us look like a giant puff pastry! Ice swans! And getting every female in our wedding party to shell out four hundred dollars for a chartreuse taffeta dress and dyed-to-match pumps that will make her look like a giant romaine lettuce and that she will never, ever wear again.

   (I'm sorry, but bridesmaid dresses are sadistic. I mean, is that really any way to treat people we love? To stage fascist, expensive photo-ops that essentially reduce everyone to a color-coordinated backdrop for our dress? I say: Give our gal-pals a break. Tell them to keep their dresses simple, and save their money for the presents.)

   Most ironically, in these scenarios the groom becomes practically irrelevant. He might as well be a doorknob.

   Given all this hoopla over the wedding being "our day," is it any wonder that we can confuse the ritual with the reality?

   A few years ago, one of the syndicated talk shows ran a feature called "Women Who Can't Stop Watching Their Wedding Videos." Many of the women on it had grown up believing that their wedding day would be "their day"—the most important day of their life.

   The problem was, their wedding day was not just "their day" but "their *only* day."

   Their wedding was really the one time when they were allowed to run the whole damn show, demand exactly what they wanted, and be the center of attention. After it was over, they were devastated. They were suddenly somebody's traditional, doormatty wife—no longer a bride or a beauty. And so they relived their wedding again and again through the VCR, trying to recapture their moment of dominion and glory.

Weddings are sacred but, hey: Every girl is entitled to more than one special day in her life. Let's make sure everyone doesn't forget this.

3. **A husband should suit our personality, not our checklist.** Years after I first paraded around as a bride, I had a boyfriend who was gung ho to get married. And if mothers could have wet dreams, let me tell you: Girls, this guy was it. The perfect mail-order groom.

He was good-looking, reliable, smart, financially secure. He was faithful, didn't drink, and actually liked going home to visit his mother each month. He wanted children and a house in the suburbs. He doted on me. He even *liked* doing laundry.

Yet, surprisingly, when he told me that he wanted to "start shopping for a ring," I felt none of the euphoria I'd always dreamed of. Instead, I felt a blood-freezing panic.

Because, while this guy was definitely a "catch," he wasn't the right catch for me. Really, I needed a far more idiosyncratic fish.

I mean, I'm my grandmother's granddaughter—and in her day, my grandmother's idea of a great catch was a Communist nymphomaniac who looked like Errol Flynn. As her prodigy, I wasn't crazy about spending every other weekend with in-laws in Cleveland and living a staid, traditional family life. Since I grew up in New York City—where you never learn to drive and therefore view all cars as a source of vehicular manslaughter—the mere idea of car-pooling kids around in a minivan made me apoplectic. And while I approached the world as a hysterical, all-you-can-eat buffet, this guy literally ate seven foods. The day he tried a scallop, it was such a big deal, you'd think he'd donated a kidney.

Our fundamental values were vastly different, our dreams were vastly different, and we couldn't negotiate any compromise.

So, difficult as it was, I told my boyfriend not to buy the ring. *Me*, the one with the doily on her head! (Interestingly enough, most of our friends assumed that *he* was the commitment-o-phobe.)

But it became clear to both of us that it's not enough to marry a list of qualities—a person who looks good on paper or seems like the "type" we're "supposed" to marry. In making a lifelong commitment to someone, we also commit to a Life. Better make sure we share the same vision.

4. **Go slow.** Funnily enough, the next guy who proposed to me was the complete opposite: a gorgeous actor-turned–gourmet chef who had businesses in Hawaii and New York. "We can spend half our time in Maui, half in Manhattan," he promised. "I can support you while you write your feminist discourse. We'll travel the world together. We'll see the great operas, eat at the greatest restaurants, and you'll have as much excitement as you've ever dreamed of!"

    Sounded great.

    There was only one problem.

    We'd been on exactly two dates.

    When I pointed out that we barely knew each other, he cried, "So what? Take a chance! Trust me, you'll love it!"—as if marrying him was akin to taking a quick spin in a Ferrari.

    Now, romance is almost, by definition, supposed to be a thing of great speed and spontaneity: a "rush," a "whirlwind" that "sweeps us off our feet" and "carries us away."

    But who the fuck has ever really enjoyed being hit by a tornado? And who the hell can think rationally in the middle of one?

    If we meet a great guy (or gal), we've got to take the time to really get to know each other and grow together—expecially if we're young.

Says my friend Dale, thirty-two, who's just gotten divorced after ten years, "When you're twenty-one, you have no idea how much you're going to grow and change in the next ten years."

Need proof? Just check out the hairdos in your high-school yearbook.

5. **Keepin' it real.** Is there anybody, among all our friends, relatives, siblings, roommates, co-workers, teachers, and lovers whom we could honestly be with 24/7 for the next fifty-eight years, who would not, on occasion, annoy the hell out of us?

Besides, for some people, finding a partner is not a matter of locking eyes with a stranger across a dance floor, but real estate: Location, location, location is everything. It's a matter of where they are in their lives, where they are in their heads, and where they both want to take things after they meet.

6. **Marriage ain't for everyone.** As Mae West once put it, "Marriage is a great institution. But I'm not ready for an institution yet."

7. **And, finally, this advice from the marrieds . . .**

   • Try to find in-laws who live in Tibet. Better yet, marry an orphan.

   • Only register for gifts at stores that will give you cash back.

   • Don't build a marriage solely on sexual chemistry. Sure, fireworks are spectacular, but look what happens to them. Fifteen seconds and *poof!*

   • Whether you hit city hall or rent out the Ritz, plan your nuptials together. Frankly, any couple that can survive planning a wedding really deserves to be together for the rest of their lives.

Chapter 12

☯

So What's Wrong with a
Little Lesbian Wedding?

---

*Saleslady at David's Bridal: "So which
one of you is the bride?"
Diane and Theresa: "We both are."*

In an ideal world, of course, I wouldn't have to write this chapter. *Unfortunately, we're a country that adores "Jerry Springer" and taking children to gun shows, but thinks that allowing gay people to build a life together is perverted. Go figure.*
  Anyway . . .
  When the United States Congress debated the so-called Marriage Protection Act back in 1996, lucky *moi* had the privilege of attending the House subcommittee hearings. The question was whether same-sex marriages should be banned on a federal level.
  Cynic that I am, I support gay marriages. This puts me in the minority, but okay. So be it. My feeling is that if any two people are actually in love (i.e., insane) enough to want to commit to spend

their entire lives together—if they're actually willing to assume legal and financial responsibility for each other until death do them part—well then, I say give 'em as much rope as they need. It's a tough, lonely life, and I don't believe in begrudging anybody a shot at some happiness and comfort. Besides, why should straight folks be the only ones who get to fill out joint income-tax forms, run up shared credit-card debt, visit each other in the intensive-care wards, and inherit each other's crappy furniture?

Gay marriage actually benefits straight gals, too. Some leaders who oppose gay marriage also support the cockamamie idea of "converting" gay men to heterosexuality. Well, as any hetero-femme can tell you, dating a closeted gay guy is no fucking picnic. Compelling homosexuals to live as straights is not doing us gals any favors. Unless both parties are *really* asexual, it's frustrating and humiliating and painful for everyone involved. Why put two people through that? The more that *all* loving partnerships can flourish in an atmosphere of truth, honesty, and acceptance, the better for everyone in the long run.

My grandmother, incidently, was a supporter of gay marriage, too—specifically, lesbian weddings. She seemed to think that lesbian weddings might be a good antidote to the man shortage in the Century Village retirement community in West Palm Beach, Florida. "So, what's wrong with a little lesbian wedding?" she once said. "I mean, what else are we elderly widows supposed to do for entertainment, once all the men have died off? This way, we could have a lot of parties and drink gin."

Congress, however, clearly doesn't share my grandmother's idea of progressive social policy.

At the time that the hearings on gay marriage took place, Newt Gingrich was riding high as the Speaker of the House. As you may guess, the proceedings were a bacchanalia of bombast, homophobia, and Bible thumping. Had the gasbags involved *not* had any real power—and had they perhaps had the imagination to speak in Monty Python accents (which make any bureaucratic proceeding infinitely more palatable)—they actually could have provided the taxpayers with a fine afternoon of comic entertainment. (I've become convinced that if we don't regard politics as a theater of the absurd, we're headed for a coronary.)

But, instead, I listened to a legion of extremely serious politicians and "experts," some of whom had a truly impressive track record of divorce and adultery themselves, testify that the "sanctity" of marriage would be destroyed if lesbians and gays were legally allowed to set up house. Apparently, heterosexual marriage only works if nobody else is allowed to copy it. According to pros such as then–California Congressman Bob Dornan, a successful marriage does not depend upon the love and commitment between the wife and husband, but upon keeping couples named Frederica and Ginger from registering for gravy boats.

Massachusetts Representative Barney Frank, bless his openly gay heart, captured this absurdity the best. At one point he asked the committee, "Are straight marriages so fragile that if me and my partner get married, it will cause your own relationships to fall apart?"

Strange as it was, a lot of people at the hearing actually seemed to think *yes*.

And this is a dirty little truth that I think deserves to be acknowledged: Policymakers seem to oppose gay marriages because they, themselves, are miserable, because their own marriages are a fragile, messy sham. Why else would they begrudge two people the right to set up an enduring partnership together? Why else would they fear their own choices will be denigrated and threatened? I mean, face it: When you're truly in love, you want the whole world to be in love with you. You feel giddy and romantic and generous. You fix people up. You're insufferably jolly—they could pour you over a waffle.

It's only when your own relationship is on the rocks, when your own sexuality is contorted and troubled, that you get miserly and mean—that you try to sabotage other couples, that you feel compelled to increase your own sense of importance through sanctimony, that you adopt the hooray-for-me, fuck-everybody-else syndrome that seems endemic to some super–right-wing conservatives.

Sure, the so-called religious activists say they're enforcing the tenets of the Bible. But the Bible (which some of us silly folks read more as a treatise on justice, love, mercy, and redemption than on retribution) has far more numerous and damning prohibitions against adultery than against homosexuality. Heck, adultery even made the Top Ten list of all God's Commandments, while the first passage that's usually cited against homosexuality remains buried somewhere in Leviticus.

And adultery is certainly far more threatening to marriage than Ellen DeGeneres and Anne Heche making kissy-kissy in Hollywood. If my husband sleeps with Mary Ann, it's far more destructive to my family than if Gilligan makes a pass at him and my husband says he isn't interested. So hel-lo? Where is the ruckus against adultery? I don't see the "family-values" folks railing against adultery nearly so much as against homosexuality. Perhaps that's because when guys like Newt Gingrich or Henry Hyde haven't been railing about the decline of family values, they've been busy cheating on their spouses.

Also, if we're going to get really literal here, the Bible also says that anyone who curses their father or mother should be put to death. Whoops! I guess there goes the entire population of teenagers! And the Bible also says: Hit your father or mother and you get put to death. Well, say sayonara to the toddlers during their terrible twos!

Of course, people like Congressman Dick Armey have insisted that they oppose homosexual marriage because gay sex is a "disease," "promiscuous," and an "unnatrual perversion."

But c'mon. Anybody who's married will tell you: Marriage ain't about sex. In fact, nothing supposedly puts the kabash on a robust sex life *faster* than marriage. I mean, we've all heard the old joke:

Q: How do you stop a girl from having sex?
A: Marry her.

So if bigots are truly opposed to gay sex, shouldn't they, more than anyone else, endorse gay marriage? I mean, what better antidote to supposed gay promiscuity? Let Adam and Steve be legally required to remain monogamous as they argue about the mortgage, then see how hot and horny they feel! Let Ada and Eve adopt a baby, then see if they still have the energy left to hit the girlie bars.

People also say they oppose gay marriage because: *Cripes! What about the children?* Children can't be allowed to see Jason with two daddies! That would send the message that gay sex is okay!

Well, let's remember one absolutely critical thing about childhood, please. Kids, no matter what their age, are absolutely loath to think about their parents—gay *or* straight—having sex.

I mean, just try thinking about it right now: *Eewwww*, right?

Nothing is more repulsive. Even if you're say, twenty-seven.

Besides, kids are narcissists. Kids believe that their parents exist for one reason only: to provide them with undivided attention twenty-four hours a day. They don't give a shit about grown-ups' sex lives. *Kids* want an audience.

If little kids do know "where babies come from," most prefer to live with the happy illusion that their parents had sex exactly the number of times it took to make them and their siblings—and no more. Orgasm, sodomy laws, homosexual feelings—all of this is *waaaay* off their radar. And this is not going to change if they have two mommies instead of one, or if "Aunt Bill" and "Uncle Bruce" take 'em to Disneyland every Christmas.

All kids really want to know is that they are not weirdos. If *Heather Has Two Mommies* is on their bookshelf, it's not going to inspire them to start imagining Mary Ann and Ginger gettin' hot 'n' heavy by the lagoon. But, if they *do* have two mommies, it may provide them with a little reassurance that *they're okay*. And this is important. Remember, when you're a kid, you can feel like an outcast if you bring meatloaf for lunch when all the other kids have bologna. It doesn't take much in second grade to earn you the nickname "Freakazoid."

Realize this, and the argument that gay marriage will "corrupt" children flies out the window, too.

No, the opposition to gay marriage is not really about sex, "religious morality," or protecting children. If you ask me, frankly, I think it's about insecurity, and maybe even a little jealousy.

Because deep, deep down in their hearts, some heterosexuals actually suspect that gay people have it easier. Sure, gay folks have to put up with violence, discrimination, and social ostracism, but hey: *They* don't have to spend the rest of their lives with members of the opposite sex.

For some straight people, heterosexuality is actually far more of a headache than they'll admit.

Yeah, there's lust and instant chemistry. But throughout history, men and women have been engaged in a holy war known as the Battle of the Sexes. To some degree, we've been raised to view each other as the enemy. Certainly, men have been encouraged to fuck as many women as possible, while women have been encouraged to "get" a man to marry us and settle down. Talk about conflicting agendas. And until very recently in the West, our roles were greatly codified religiously, socially, economically, and sexually—and grossly unequal. In most places, they still are.

Plus, men and women often perceive each other as predatory and alien. I mean, why else would *Men Are from Mars, Women Are from Venus* become a bestseller? Why else are there humorous self-help books advising women to use dog-training techniques on their boyfriends? Just try selling something like that to lesbians. Hell, try selling *The Rules* to lesbians. Or take the De Beers TV commercial for a diamond engagement ring. It shows the silhouette of a man who is getting ready to place an enormous rock on his fiancée's finger—his fiancée whom the ad describes as an exquisitely "incomprehensible creature." Oh boy. *An incomprehensible creature.* Just whom *I'd* want to spend the rest of my life with.

And listen to straight people in bars.

The guys: "Augh! Women! You can't live with 'em, you can't live without 'em! We will *never* understand women."

And from the girls: "Guys are dogs. They will never be like your girlfriends. So you've got to remember not to expect too much."

Add to this the fact that our sexual peaks are separated by eighteen years, and our sexual responsiveness is vastly different, and it's a miracle that men and women have gotten together at all in the past fifteen thousand years. And yet, to this very day, we're expected to build lifelong partnerships together. We're told, in fact, that the very foundation of our society and the future of our species depends upon it. Oh. Great. No pressure there.

So, when I hear straight guys being homophobic assholes, what I really hear is envy. Beneath their words, I hear their resentment and frustration over having to relate to us chicks. It's like: *Hey, we have to put up with those stupid bitches, with all their nagging and irrational demands and expectations. We have to try and be macho but also keep our pants zipped and watch our mouths and worry about pissin' them off. We can't have sex with whomever we want, wherever we want—at least without paying a price for it. Why the hell should the gay guys get off so easy? They want the benefits of being married? Let 'em marry a chick, like I did!*

And when I hear straight women denigrate lesbians, the subtext I often hear is their own dissatisfaction with men: *Hey, of course I'd prefer to share a household with my friend Sharon, who really understands me—rather than this King of Flatulence who watches football all day and whose idea of a romantic gesture is to change the oil in my Subaru. But we all make compromises. Why can't these women get with the program the way I did?*

And listening to the right-wing wackos at the gay-marriage hearings, this is what I heard, too: fear and jealousy and romantic dissatisfaction. And so did my man Barney Frank.

Not that any of this justifies rampant heterosexism, gay-bashing, or discrimination, of course.

But the way I see it, when it comes to combating discrimination, any insights into the opposition can be a real power tool.

So next time some moron rails against "lezzies and perverts" getting married, I say we just go, "Wow. Your own love life must suck. Otherwise, you wouldn't be so threatened by anyone else's."

This could stun them into a silence. Or make them vein-popping mad. Either way: points for our team.

I suppose we could remind them, too, that committed gay couples are actually no different from straight couples in the long run. Long-term relationships all have their hopes and disappointments, neuroses and challenges. Nobody is immune to heartache.

But nah. Let 'em suffer. Let their own fear and ignorance work against 'em. Let 'em believe deep down inside that lesbians really *do* have it better.

Chapter 13

ꝏ

We *Are* the Fashion Police

Laugh and the world laughs with you.
Cry and you cry with your girlfriends.
—LAURIE KUSLANSKY

I recently attended a women's networking dinner in Virginia where a bevy of very hip, very multicultural, very accomplished professional gals sat around discussing—you guessed it—golf.

That's right, golf. As in: the game that mostly white guys with zero fashion sense play. As in: take the stick, hit the ball, and try to get it in the hole—eighteen fucking times in a row. As in: *Zzzzzzzzz* . . .

Golf holds only one point of interest for me, and that's the caddy. Get some hot young college buck to follow me around schlepping my stuff, and hey, we can talk. Thing is, he'll have to do this off the green, too. (In fact, here's an idea for "family-values" advocates who tee off every Sunday: If they really want to help American families, why not send their caddies to help out new parents once in a while? Goddess knows that a new mom could use an extra pair of helping hands.)

But anyway: While none of the women at the dinner were under the illusion that golf was actually *interesting*, more than a few had discovered that learning to play golf constituted a serious career move.

Said a woman named Diane, who'd launched her own business, "I've discovered that all the deals are being cut on the fairway, not in the boardroom. If I want to play with the Big Boys, I have to play golf with them."

"It's what the men in my office play, too," said a woman named Charlie, in dreadlocks. "If you want to get ahead, it helps to be a golfer."

And so, in the middle of the dinner party, these women began trading notes on stuff like titanium-headed drivers, nine-irons, and mulligans.

Dear Goddess. Couldn't we just fuck our way to the top like we used to?

Look, we women need a *serious* Old Girls' Network—and we need it fast. Otherwise, we're going to have to spend our lives kissing up to the good ol' boys by playing golf—a game that's so dumb, players actually brag about their handicaps.

We gals need some serious, universal methods of female bonding—personally and professionally. Yeah, the term *sisterhood* inspires some eye rolling among us cynical chicks. After all, we know that sisters can claw each other's eyes out over the last piece of blueberry pie just as easily as they can share it. Unlike our feminist foremothers, we're under no illusions: Just because somebody has a twat doesn't automatically mean she's our ally.

We know how hard women can be on each other. My grandma, in fact, used to say that we women are harder on each other than anybody else—and in some cases, Girl, ain't that the truth.

From Day One in the playground, girls police each other with a ferocity that's better suited to a gulag than to a swing set. "Eew, Donna's wearing purple! Eew! Melissa drinks tomato juice! Eew! Keisha's playing with the pigeons! Eew! Look everybody!" This establishes a Greek chorus of social judgment that may get tempered with age but that can last, frankly, until our funerals. ("Good God! She chose to be buried in *that*?")

It's not just professional misogynists like Joan Rivers or Phyllis Schlafly who bat against the home team. Plenty of good-hearted gals take swings at other women without even realizing it:

If I had thighs as big as that woman's, they say, *I would not be wearing biking shorts.*

Ouch. That woman's do is sooo twenty years ago.

Somebody should tell her that miniskirts are no longer cute on someone her age.

We women are only too highly attuned to whose shoes work with her outfit, to who's having a bad hair day, to who's gained six pounds and is wearing fake breasts. As a comedian wrote in "One Hundred Reasons Why It's Great to Be a Guy," "When you're a guy, old friends don't give a crap if you've lost or gained weight." Well, we gals have seen the Fashion Police and, frankly, it is us.

But we all know the importance of "playing for the girl's team," too. We know the power, the glory, and the thrill of connecting with other women. And it comes so naturally. Hell, all we have to do is wait on line to pee in a public ladies' room. Suddenly: Voilà, it's girls' night out. In the fifteen minutes it takes women to move from the hallway of the cineplex to the three piddly stalls by the Tampax machine, we can learn each other's life stories. We'll tell each other about our bastard ex-boyfriend, our menstrual cramps, and the factory outlet where we got this groovy outfit. While washing our hands, we can have meaningful conversations about acupuncture or breast-feeding with women we've never met before. While applying lipstick, we can compare notes about Pap smears with absolute strangers. And if the toilets are out of order, forget it! An entire feminist revolution can be forged around a paper-towel dispenser. We're our own portable war council, complete with extra Kleenex.

Unlike men, who seem to "bond" the way steel girders bond— only through intense heat, external pressure, and a degree of contortion—women "connect." Studies have shown that most men do not make new close friends after the age of twenty-five. Not so for us. Intimacy comes as easily as, well, peeing.

But our relationships with other women do require care and feeding. And it's always struck me as odd that our culture gives us plenty of handy rules for catching a husband, rules for dieting, and rules for investing. But when it comes to friendship—and how to treat other women with respect—we're left to improvise.

I mean, obviously, we girls all know not to sleep with our best friend's lover, or even our best friend's ex-lover. And unless we both agree to it beforehand, true friends do not wear the same outfit to the same party.

But wouldn't it be useful to establish some guidelines beyond this, for ways in which we women should treat each other in general? A universal code of decency among women, perhaps, to help us foster a greater, stronger sense of camaraderie? I mean, we can only hang out in the bathroom for so long. And while a Room of One's Own is important—especially in a Man's World—it would be nice to have a place that doesn't consist mainly of toilets and those annoying, eternally broken hand driers.

So, for starters, why don't we promote these New Rules for Girls?

1. **Friends shouldn't be treated as leftovers.** You know: taken out and heated up only when there's nothing fresh around? Face it, nothing is so insulting and infuriating as a girlfriend who drops out of sight the moment a Love Interest appears on her horizon. Because the message she sends to her pink posse is: You are only worthwhile when there's no man around. You are *grout*. You are a consolation prize. You are a backup singer.

   Unfortunately, whenever the great romance finally hits some bumps in the road (and all romances do—it comes with the territory) this Invisible Woman usually reappears, seeking the love and support of the very gal-pals she abandoned. And this makes for a great deal of resentment, tension, and mistrust: *Oh, now you call us. Where were you when you weren't unhappy and needy?*

Why create this situation? If we can be conscientious about keeping up our hair and nails, certainly we can do the same with our friends. Yeah, romance is heady and love is blind. But this doesn't justify treating our friends like chopped liver. If we can manage to pay our bills during the first crazy days of passion, or even pick up a carton of milk once a week, surely we can pick up the phone, send an e-mail, and show a little R-E-S-P-E-C-T to the people who have been with us through hangovers, makeovers, and sleepovers for years.

2. **Don't dis the sisters.** Unless they treat us badly, let's not make a sport out of putting down other women. If a babe weighs three hundred pounds and has decided to wear pink Spandex hot pants, hey: All power to her! If another babe has men swarming around her like the floor of the stock market, so okay. Good for her. We may feel inadequate in comparison for a moment or two, but we'll get over it. We're goddesses in our own right and we'll have our own days in the sun.

   If a female boss is assertive and short tempered, don't join other colleagues in branding her a bitch. A mother with three whiny children slows down the checkout line at the Food Lion? Offer to give her a hand instead of rolling our eyes. And if we see a woman in a fabulous dress or with beautiful hair, let's tell her! It won't cost us anything, and it'll generate a little kindness and kinship in a world full of misogyny.

   We need to cut our gender some *serious* slack, beyond the folksingers and Girl Power T-shirts. We have nothing to gain by judging, back-stabbing, or criticizing each other unnecessarily. But we do have everything to lose.

3. **Keep our hands off another girl's honey.** Sometimes it's hard to resist, I know. But we shouldn't kid ourselves: It's wrong to knowingly sleep with another woman's husband, no matter what *he* tells us about the marriage, no matter if he's a rock star, a millionaire, or the president. It's not "just between the guy and his wife." Besides, let's not flatter ourselves: Seducing married guys is no victory. They're actually far easier targets than the unmarried ones.

4. **Toot each other's horns.** Oscar Wilde once said, "Every time a friend succeeds, a little something inside me dies." Ain't that the awful truth. Sometimes, if a friend wins, say, a Guggenheim Fellowship or finds a rent-stabilized apartment in New York City, their bliss becomes our misery.

Conversely, our friends' misery can also become our bliss: *Yippee. Sheila's credit rating is worse than my own. Ho boy, I sure am glad I don't have genital warts. Hee hee, too bad about Trudy and her boyfriend. How was she supposed to know he meant "sophomore" in high school?*

Yeah, well, whenever possible, we gals should ignore our jealous little hearts and toot each other's horns instead. Frankly, if we don't promote each other and cheerlead for *ourselves*, few others will.

Besides, fifteen years from now we may not remember the pangs of jealousy we felt when our colleague landed a kick-ass promotion, but *she* may very well remember how we sprang for a bottle of bubbly, led the office in a toast, and gave her major props. And what goes around comes around: Let's start our engines and spread that good karma.

5. **Network like maniacs.** All those middle-aged guys in suits who brag about being "self-made" men have a vast network of loved ones, fraternity brothers, golf buddies, Elks, Lions, alumni, and underlings to thank. So we women are wise to build similar networks and clubhouses of our own.

Since we dames tend to love a little dinner party anyway, why not make our social lives do double duty? Regular Girls' Nights Out and potlucks can be a networking tool. Ditto for going to sporting events in which *women* are playing, thank you.

Or, perhaps better still, we can throw bimonthly "business dinners," featuring demonstration parties for stuff like Tupperware, the Pampered Chef, Mary Kay, Weekenders, and so forth. These companies tend to be comprised mainly of *saleswomen* who work on commission—and who will come right to our homes for a demo. This way we get to (a) eat, (b) shop,

(c) support another woman running *her* own business, and, (d) network all at the same time. I mean, short of a couple of orgasms, what could be better?

Recently in Nashville, Tennessee, a group of women writers formed the League of Beleaguered Women (shouldn't we have a spin-off, the Beleaguered Women Voters?) in order to lend each other support in what is generally—trust me on this—a thankless and frustrating profession.

Well, their name got me thinking: Since the right wing often appropriates the language of patriotism and domesticity for its extremist, patriarchal organizations (i.e., Focus on the Family, the Eagle Forum, the Heritage Foundation), thus making a mockery of all that is good, why not respond in kind by giving our networks names that spoof the right? We could form the Wiccan Coalition. The Goddess Squad. Onward Vixen Soldiers. The Tea 'n' Crumpet Strumpets. You get the idea.

6. **Great Expectations is a work of fiction.** If a guy washes our dishes one night, lets us control the TV remote, and calls when he says he's going to call, we think he's a saint. If he says excuse-me after he burps and puts the toilet seat down, we think he deserves the Congressional Medal of Honor. If he knows how to make spaghetti without reading the directions on the side of the box, we think he's a domestic genius. But let our girlfriend go a week without returning our phone calls and, forget it, she's in the doghouse.

Hel-lo?

7. **Avoid the "chicken-dinner syndrome."** My friend Ophi has an expression called the "chicken-dinner syndrome." That's when women pick ourselves apart like a chicken dinner, critiquing our thighs, legs, breasts, and so forth in an orgy of self-hatred until we've virtually cut ourselves to pieces.

Well, I've seen chicken-dinner syndrome on a communal level as well, and it ain't any prettier. In this case, one woman takes the floor at a conference, heads a business meeting, or otherwise speaks her mind—and the other women in the audience promptly pick her apart. Everyone takes a piece of her until there's nothing left.

I've watched a female office staff verbally hack apart a female boss because they didn't like the Christmas presents she gave them. (Never mind that her predecessor, a man, gave out bupkus for six years running.) I've heard single mothers tell a congresswoman—who was working to protect their interests from budget cuts—"Well, I'm not voting for you because you're just fat and ugly." And I've heard women dis a brilliant female professor because her clothes were a little, shall we say, unfortunate.

Obviously, we shouldn't brainwash ourselves with estrogen. There's no glory in supporting women just because they're women. But would it kill us to give each other the benefit of the doubt once in a while?

Remember, we need each other. When our panties are down and there's no more toilet paper in the ladies' room, it's the woman in the next stall we're always going to turn to for help.

Chapter 14

ⓒⓞ

Wisdom from Dickville

You can admire Clint Eastwood without starving yourself to look like him.
—"ONE HUNDRED REASONS WHY IT'S GREAT TO BE A GUY"

Women have spent a fair amount of time these past thirty years debating The Man Question—namely, how we liberated gals can and should relate to our XY-chromosomed counterparts. Yet if you're reading this chapter in the hope of learning how to catch a player *or* conquer the patriarchy, *fageddaboutit.* I won't be offering any pointers on how to win men's hearts *or* cut off their balls. There are other books for that. Besides, I can't tell you how to best deal with men because, frankly, I'm still figuring it out myself. And I suspect it's going to take a really long time. Like, say, seventy years. Yeah, this is depressing, but let's think of it this way: As much as we gals cannot, for the life of us, figure out how to relate to guys, they, for the life of them, cannot figure out how to relate to us. So who says there's not an iota of sexual justice in this world?

Instead, I'd like to use this chapter to outline what I think we can *learn* from men—the regular Joes—the straight guys who fall somewhere between Jerry Falwell and Jerry Springer.

Stop laughing. I'm serious.

Look, I know that if most guys had their way, they'd use the federal-budget surplus to make the tits bigger on the Statue of Liberty. But for the moment, at least, I'm willing to look beyond that.

Because the battle of the sexes is like nuclear war. Nobody can possibly really win it. I mean, if we can't get it together, who the hell else are we going to talk to on this planet? Parrots?

Besides, truth be told, I actually have great hopes for men and women of today. Date rape, gangsta rap, and sexual miscommuniqués aside, we've also grown up as *friends* in ways that perhaps no other American generations have before.

Thanks to sex ed, coed dormitories, our hyper-confessional culture, the blurring of traditional gender roles, Title IX, and even the epidemic of divorce (which often made our *parents* the common enemy), we boys and girls are comfortable around the opposite sex in ways that our parents simply weren't.

Just check out our college dorm rooms. Check out the apartments we share. Hell, check out the TV shows we watch, such as *Friends* and *The Real World*. These wouldn't have existed back in 1962. The central premise was simply not a reality.

Back when my folks were in college, the relationship between men and women was largely a wrestling match—a covert war. The girls tried to trick the boys into marrying them, and the boys tried to trick the girls into fucking them. People didn't attempt to understand each other; mystifying gender differences were deliberately exaggerated.

And while a twenty-first century crybaby like Wendy Shalit has written a whole book bemoaning the loss of sexual naivete, you won't find me endorsing it. In the long run, I think the fact that today's *garçons et filles* are not *completely* bamboozled by each other bodes well for both sexes and all sexual orientations.

Frankly, I think it's healthier to know boys as poignant, horny, human dorks than as some enigmatic, war-mongering, lecherous Other. And I think it's healthier that boys see me as a sentient, passionate, fallible human than as some scheming, incomprehensible sprite with a pussy. I mean, just because sexual difference exists doesn't mean we have to be morons about it.

Big-hearted optimistic babe that I am, I believe that if we're open, we can learn from each other. There may even be some stuff we gals can learn from the guys.

I'm not serving up refried beans here: I'm not advocating that women play like men or try to be just like them. We tried that before, and mostly it resulted in unfortunate stuff like "power bows" and being casualties in "fuck-and-run" incidents. Nor am I suggesting we become Eliza Doolittles to their Henry Higginses.

Rather, I think we gals might be able to cultivate some more power for ourselves by mimicking guys in terms of what they *do not* do.

Face it, there are some self-defeating behaviors that guys refuse to indulge in. And if we could do a little figurative cross-dressing in these areas, a little gender-bending in the Attitude Department, it might do us prima donnas a world of good. Not only that, but there's a fabulous irony in strengthening girls by appropriating the healthy habits of the boys.

For example, consider the following:

1. **Men do not apologize to inanimate objects.** (Granted, I've heard it said that men don't apologize to anyone, but hey, nobody's perfect.) Have you ever seen a woman bump into a chair and say to the chair, "Oops, I'm sorry"? I've seen women say "excuse me" to wastepaper baskets. I've seen women say "pardon me" to table legs. On occasion, I've seen women apologize to extension cords, department-store mannequins, and packing crates that people have left in the middle of their living rooms. Once I even watched a woman do a mea culpa to a parking cone.

   To this end, I have also seen someone with a huge duffle bag bump into a woman and almost knock her down. And I've seen the woman—not the walker—say, "Oh! I'm sorry." Wherever I go, I see gals constantly striving to be polite, game, and invisible. I hear us excuse ourselves for living.

"I'm sorry! Pardon me, let me move my small children, their stroller, and all my grocery bags so you can wedge in here with your golf clubs."

We exhibit such continual discomfort in the world; we're so nervous and conditioned to assume we're wrong, that we apologize anytime there's a gaff—even if this means we end up apologizing to the radiator.

And, let me tell you, this is not one of our more attractive qualities.

Guys don't do this. When a guy trips over a packing crate, you know what he does? He curses. He goes, "Who the fuck put this box here?"—even if he left it there himself.

2. **Men do not schlepp.** Men do not routinely carry their lunch in a plastic shopping bag along with a gym bag and a purse slung across their chest like a bandolier containing, among other things, a makeup bag, a Toni Morrison novel, a bottle of Nuprin, Certs, Q-tips in a baggie, six Tampons, a comb, a checkbook, a Dayrunner, seventeen ATM receipts, a Lady Speed Stick, a curling iron, and a Powerbar.

Unless they're working out, most men will not even carry a bottle of spring water.

Men understand the value of being as physically unencumbered as possible. After all, how free can you be if your hands and shoulders aren't?

Yeah, women's clothes often don't have pockets (which I'm convinced is a conspiracy by clothing manufacturers to sell us more purses, and thus more clothes to go with them). But how much stuff do we actually need with us at all times? *Schlepping is not a source of female empowerment.* We can't be liberated if we're bogged down with crappola 24/7.

So let's take a page from the boys on this one. Men do not buy bags that they have to carry in other bags. I say: Let's use a man's wallet, take our keys, a lipstick, some Kleenex, and be done with it. (Our arms and shoulders will say, "amen, sister," too.)

3. **Men do not wear shoes they can't walk in.** Wanna stand on your own two feet? Then be able to stand on your own two feet. We gals are not going to be able to get to the top in this world if we can't walk there, let alone run. Men understand this; their idea of a great shoe is one that feels so good they forget they're even wearing it. (Bonus points if the insoles don't smell.) I'm not saying we've got to invest in Birken-stock (ugh), but, face it, if we say, "These boots are made for walkin'," then hobble away, trip over the rug, and fall flat on our face, how empowering is *that*?

4. **For men, dressing rooms are for trying on clothes, not contemplating surgery.** Do you think men would squeeze themselves into jock straps that cut off their circulation? If a fashion magazine told men that "Big dicks are *out* this year. Teeny peenies are *in!*" do you think for one moment they'd start hating themselves if they were well endowed? If men were told that the only way they could fit into this season's pants was to weigh one hundred pounds and have tiny testicles, do you think they'd consider plastic surgery or go running to the gym? Pul-leze.

    When it comes to fashion, guys know a moronic idea when they see one. (Okay, maybe not when it comes to *hats*, but remember Donna Karan's "skirts for men" a few years back? If you don't, it's only further proof of how quickly those got the thumbs-down.)

    Men also don't spend their hard-earned bucks on threads that don't fit, hoping they'll be able to "diet into them." They don't have a "dream suit" that they "just have to squeeze into or they'll die!" You won't hear guys say, "I'm a forty-four long, but I swear I'm going to make it into a thirty-eight regular." They know that's physically impossible, and they accept that. They have an innate, zenlike understanding that clothes are supposed to fit you, not vice versa.

    So next time we're shopping, if we can't find anything that fits us right, it'll do us gals some good to think like a guy and get ourselves to a good seamstress, not a plastic surgeon. Fabric, not flesh, was meant to be altered.

5. **Men do not call the psychic hotline for career advice.**
Nor do they read their horoscopes in the newspaper every day to see how the stars will affect their relationship. Nor do they buy candles, rocks, or soaps that promise to "empower" them.

If they do get their tarot cards read by a person at a street fair, nine times out of ten they're the kind of guys who played Dungeons & Dragons in high school.

Recently I received a catalog full of "gifts to inspire and celebrate women."

Among the pickings? "Prosperity candles." Apparently, we're supposed to "light prosperity candles while paying bills, making money decisions, and plotting business strategies"—though exactly how plunking down forty-nine dollars for three shafts of green wax will help *us* financially is unclear. (Plus, is it ever a good idea to fill out our tax returns by candlelight? Don't bank on it.)

Other "pro-woman" gifts? To "encourage your highest aspirations," there are "dream" and "wish" pillows (are we supposed to sleep our way to the top?). "Goddess nail potion," apparently "a powerful tool to remind you to embrace your true magnificence." (Don't embrace too hard, though. You might chip your manicure.) And "ritual for success" boxes containing incense, "success oil," herbs, flowers, a charm pouch, and a "magic knot chord." Oh, great. Just the thing we need to win us that big fat promotion—a New Age noose.

I mean, c'mon. Guys will not buy this crap. And for good reason.

Look, I'm all for tapping the unseen forces of the universe. I'm an astrology buff myself, and I'll be the first to agree that some phenomena exist that can't been seen or proven. Faith, magic, the paranormal: sure. Why not? Power to the powers.

For that matter, I'm all for women selling whimsical crafts through a catalog, too. But let's not confuse entrepreneurism with hucksterism. And let's not kid each other that there's career power in patchouli or cold hard cash in a candle. We don't become more successful by painting our nails "Athena Purple." I know some real witches and, trust me, they don't get their power through a mail-order catalog.

Likewise, plunking down our hard-earned shekels on a 900 number does not make us the mistress of our own fate. It makes us mental Cinderellas, hoping a fairy godmother will work her magic, use her crystal ball, and do the rescue work for us. Success ain't achieved by manipulating unseen forces—it's achieved through our own damn hard work.

Sure, leaders like Napoleon and Ronald Reagan had astrologers counseling them. But these guys also had vast armies and empires at their disposal.

So, when it comes to quick-fix psychics, potions, and simplistic starcasts, sisters take heed: Make sure your head isn't so far in Uranus that you really can't function down here on Earth.

6. **If men crave a chocolate bar, they don't eat fourteen rice cakes.** Plus a bag of carrot sticks, some leftover chicken, and a bowl of Tofutti—then break down and eat the chocolate bar anyway, hating themselves for it the whole time.

Men are stunningly direct in their needs. When they're hungry, they eat. When they want a cheeseburger, they eat a cheeseburger. When they want ice cream, they say, "Hey, I want some ice cream." They don't go, "Hey, does anyone here want ice cream?" then stew if nobody else does because now it means they can't have some, either.

And this modus operandi of theirs extends beyond food. Men are not afraid to ask for what they want, period, for fear that "nobody will like them." Whether they're asking a secretary to write a letter for them, a waiter to take back a lousy steak, or their boss for a raise, they express their needs clearly and directly. And, big surprise, they tend to get what they want more frequently than women who hem and haw, hoping the world will "get it."

7. **When men go on diets, they don't make a career out of it.** They don't buy calorie counters, tiny food scales, and join support groups with weekly weigh-ins en masse in which they discuss "strategies for holiday eating." Doctors—or significant others—tell men what they can and cannot eat, and the guys pretty much take it from there.

   At restaurants, they shrug their shoulders and say to the waitress, "Nope. Can't eat burgers. Doctor says I can't have red meat. Guess I'll have the heart-smart fish-fiesta platter." Then they shrug their shoulders, pat their bellies, and say, "Yep, I'm getting a gut. Guess I have to cut back on the beer and do a little NordicTrak." When we ask them how much weight they want to lose, they shrug their shoulders again: "I dunno. Coupla pounds. Enough so I can fit back into my jeans." End of story. The next forty-five minutes are not spent in an orgy of self-flagellation and calorie parsing.

8. **Men do not insist upon HTA (Home Toilet Advantage).** Okay, I know this isn't ladylike, but if we're going to talk about improving women's lives, at some point we've got to mention "going to the bathroom." I don't like it either. I'm as prissy as they come when it's time to visit the Scatology Department.

   But let's face it, most gals I know would sooner throw up in somebody else's bathroom than use it for anything more than a quick pee. (I mean, the doo-doo taboo is so pervasive that "Sex and the City" once based an entire episode around the fact that Sarah Jessica Parker's character finally "did a number two" in her boyfriend's bathroom.) Granted, the lines in ladies' rooms are long enough, but I know women who are so uncomfortable doing their business in *any* other bathroom (i.e., dorm, office, in-laws) that they develop some serious gastrointestinal problems. Men will take a dump anywhere—and their bathroom lines are still shorter and faster (go figure). To that end, men also do not refuse to pee in the middle of a romantic moment for fear of "ruining the mood." Perhaps this is one of the *many* reasons they get fewer bladder infections than we do.

For the sake of our health, we may be wise to take a cue from them and, ahem, lighten up a little.

Anyhow, these are small things, I know. But in their own way, they have the potential to improve how comfortable we feel in our own skin and in the world at large. And the beauty of it is, while we're learning these behaviors from guys, it absolutely in no way interferes with guys learning stuff from us.

And what might this stuff be?

Oh, just about everything else in the world that's not on this list.

Chapter 15

୧୨

Family. Oy.
How to Survive Your Relatives

I was on a corner the other day when a
wild-looking sort of gypsy lady with
a dark veil over her face grabbed me
on Ventura Boulevard and said, "Karen
Haber! You're never going to find
happiness, and no one is ever going
to marry you." I said, "Mom, leave
me alone."

—KAREN HABER

They begin in November, just before Thanksgiving, and their symptoms usually last until a few days after New Year's. I'm speaking, of course, about those dreaded winter afflictions known as *parentus horriblus, siblingus tensus,* and *relativus overloadus,* otherwise known as "holidays with your family."

"Well, I'm off to Bosnia," my co-worker Jamie groans. "Bosnia" refers not to the former Yugoslavia but to her parents' house in New Jersey, where her mother stops chain-smoking just long enough to say things to Jamie like, "Tell that no-good father of yours to pass the fucking latkes."

Mariel calls me. "*That Woman* just telephoned again to ask why I'm not coming to Boca a day early to help her clean the garage. One more call from *That Woman* and, I swear, I'm joining the Hari Krishnas."

That Woman, by the way, is what Mariel calls her mother.

Then my girl Barbara drops by. "Guess what I'm getting for Christmas?" she announces. "A new stepmother. Dad's girlfriend number three. The one who's two years younger than me and works at the roller rink. Got any Prozac?"

"Time to spend Thanksgiving with the Mouth from the South," groans my friend Chris, referring to her sister. "Five days of listening to her brag about how much her furniture costs."

Aah, family.

Face it, anyone who advocates "traditional family values" has obviously never spent any quality time with their relatives. If they did, they'd realize that most people's families are such a Piece of Work, they deserve their own patent. They'd see that Tolstoy was basically dyslexic. It's not that "each unhappy family is unhappy in its own way." It's that, in their own way, each family is capable of making us, personally, really, really miserable.

If you disagree, by the way, you can stop reading this chapter immediately and climb back on your spaceship.

Sure, it's comforting to have a group of people who are either genetically or legally required to look out for us. And sure, they can, on occasion, provide unparalleled strength and comfort. But let's face a few facts here. First of all, most families today are shaken—not blended. And on a day-to-day basis, when everybody is in okay health and there aren't any disasters looming, the traditional family values that most folks practice are things like Nagging and Silent Treatment, Guilt and Fighting Over the Check. Yelling and Paying Backhanded Compliments Like That New Haircut Looks Good It Really Hides Your Double Chin.

Nothing, but nothing, can shred a girl's self-esteem as easily as our families can.

Forget high school. No one rattles our cool, fuels our insecurities, criticizes us, or makes us revert back to an eager-to-please seven-year-old more quickly than our relatives. Even when they aren't around, we feel perpetually watched and judged by them. They're perched on our shoulders like those angels and devils in the cartoons—our father in a red catsuit with horns and a pitchfork; our mother in a white tutu, a lopsided halo bobbing over her head—everyone who's ever raised us hovering above us in a choir of critics whispering:

That's what you're wearing?

It's about time you cleaned your apartment.

So when are you going to find someone nice and settle down already?

You know, something like that is no longer cute at your age.

This is the dirty little secret that's so often ignored by traditional feminism: The patriarchy may promote all sorts of sexism, but often these values are instilled in us not by Rush Limbaugh but by our mother's holier-than-thou sister Darlene whose unofficial mantra is, "Keep acting like that and you'll never get a husband."

We don't learn gender-role stereotypes from the Southern Baptist Convention, *Playboy*, or Phyllis Schlafly. We get them from a catty, competitive older sister who announces, "*I'm* the pretty one. *You* just have personality." Or a father who routinely tells us to "go help grandma" in the kitchen while he and our brothers watch the Super Bowl. Or a mother who says, "If Jeffrey is hitting you in the playground, that's just because he likes you."

The sad truth is that the people who share our home turf, if not our DNA, can do more damage to a gal's sense of personal power than all those fartbags at the Heritage Foundation combined.

Recently, I attended a women's forum lead by Regina Williams, chairwoman of the Michigan chapter of the National Association to Advance Fat Acceptance (NAAFA). The young women in the audience were of all ethnicities and backgrounds, but, truth be told, Williams was the only sister in the room who clocked in at three hundred pounds. Interestingly enough, she was also the only sister in the room who'd posed for a magazine in a leopard-skin bathing suit (but that's another story).

Compared to her, the rest of us looked svelte, as my grandmother used to say. Nonetheless, when Williams asked us, "How many of you think you're overweight?" at least eighty percent of us raised our hands.

"Now, to me, all of you appear to be of average weight," Williams said. "Where do you get the idea that you're heavy?"

The obvious answer, of course, would have been the media. And at first, I admit, we gals indulged in a little Calvin and *Cosmo* bashing. But then the majority of us began talking about our families. And talking. And talking. It didn't take Buffy to find the real demons.

"Every time I go home for the holidays I tense up," one woman confessed. "I know that as soon as I walk in the door and take off my coat, my mother's going to give me the once-over. She won't even have to say anything. I'll know just from the way she raises one eyebrow that she thinks I've gained weight."

"I have three brothers, and we all have hearty appetites," said another. "But my stepfather always makes these snide remarks at the dinner table, like, 'Wow, look at her shovel it in. She's a regular John Deere backhoe.'"

"Every family get-together becomes a search-and-destroy mission," said a third, who identified herself as an artist. "First they ask me why I'm so heavy. Why haven't I been taking care of myself, they ask. When I tell them I'm fine, they say, 'How can you be fine working at Starbucks?' I say that Starbucks is great—it covers my health insurance and gives me time to paint. Then my uncle goes something like 'Paint, *schmaint*. You can't pay your rent with a picture, you know.' At which point, my mother always jumps in and says how I should be in law school. Lawyers make *real money*, she says. And then, my aunt adds something about how all the good single men are in law school—maybe I'd *finally* get a boyfriend. At which point, of course, the discussion comes full circle, because then my mother says, 'But who's going to want to date you when you're so fat?'"

What's a girl to do? Intellectually, of course, we may realize that our families' criticisms of us are not actually about us, but *them*—their life choices, their disappointments, their hopes and fears, and so forth. Yet this is cold comfort when our *own* demons start emerging after Halloween each year. I mean, it's one thing to know that your family is a tin of assorted nuts like everybody else's. It's quite another *not* to let them actually sap us of our confidence.

How do modern chicks rule the world when we feel cowed in our own roost? How do we recuperate from our relatives?

For those who find comfort in "misery loves company," there are always twelve-step programs—guaranteed to introduce us to at least one family more insane that our own. And if we can swing therapy, hey, I was born in New York City, so of course I'm going to recommend it to every SmartMouth Goddess. Unlike the rest of the nation, we white broads from New York think something's wrong with people if they *don't* have a shrink.

But what if we don't have the time, money, or inclination to spend years "working out our issues" so that we can "finally get to a secure place," so that we can eventually spend a holiday with our lover or eat a piece of cheesecake without hearing the Greek chorus of our relatives condemning our decisions?

Or what if we realize that making peace with our parents can take a lifetime, and since we have only one life to live, we'd rather spend it pursuing more realistic goals?

For those of us who'd like some nontraditional ways of dealing with traditional dilemmas, read on.

1. **Be a smartass.** At least once when we're little (which means, as far as our parents are concerned, anytime before we turn fifty), every single one of us hears the phrase, "Don't you open up a big fresh mouth to me, young lady." Variations of this include such classics as, "Don't you be sassin' me," "Don't you talk to your mother like that," and "One more word like that and I'll wash your mouth out with Palmolive."

Being a SmartMouth is clearly kin to guerrilla warfare. Which is exactly why we might entertain it as an option. Desperate situations call for desperate measures.

Next time we're bombarded with sexist, busybody, and unsolicited comments from our relatives, we should try opening up that big fresh mouth we've always been told to keep shut. If we're lucky, we may shock or enrage folks enough to make them stop talking to us. Make a habit out of such sarcasm and who knows? We might spend years of being ignored! Consider the following handy responses to frequent and annoying comments:

Comment: So, when are you going to get a real job?

A. Hey, what's not "real" about lap dancing?

B. Well, my boss says that if I continue to be "nice" to him after hours, I'll never have to work again.

C. How about when Uncle Artie gets a real toupee?

Comment: Still not married, hmmm?

A. Nah, just sleeping around.

B. Well, my boyfreind is, so the way I see it, we're one-for-one.

C. No, but the baby's due in May

Comment: You've put on weight.

A. Yeah, great sex'll do that to you.

B. Good. I'll have more to throw around.

C. Let's hope so. Last time you saw me, I was six.

Comment: You're not getting any younger.

A. I know. That's why my lovers are!

B. True, but look at the bright side: At the rate you're aging, *you* could be back in diapers soon.

C. Gosh, you say that like it's a *bad* thing.

Comment: So, when are you planning on giving me grand-children?

A. I don't know. When are you planning on breaking a hip?

B. How's about after you leave me a big inheritance?

C. Not until I get a cute girlfriend and a really good turkey baster.

2. **Regard your family as a source of popular entertainment.** There's a reason situation comedies are often built around families. What other human unit is such fertile ground for bad one-liners and theater of the absurd?

If it's hard to get any distance from your family's neuroses, try pretending they're on television. Write wacky character descriptions for them in your head, such as: Cousin Harriet, the Queen of Thorazine. Uncle Levar, the Man Who Insists He Could've Won the Lottery If It Wasn't for the Goddamn Communists. Psycho Cousin Elwood, Who's Making a Suspension Bridge out of String in His Bedroom.

Nothing like reducing our loved ones to caricatures to make them bearable.

Or, alternately, you might try teaming up with a trusted sibling or cousin to hold a secret Family Olympics.

Decide in advance what the categories will be. My personal favorites are Competitive Nagging (it has to contain at least five minutes of unmitigated nudging); the Long-Distance Guilt Call ("Me? I'm not lonely. Not that you would know."); Track Discussion (when people belabor the same issue over and over): and Thin-Ice Skating (mentioning any touchy subject).

Take mental notes during the course of the visit. Then, whenever you and your cohorts can sneak away for a few moments, judge your relatives' performance in the various categories:

"I give Uncle Tyron a 5.7 in the Track Discussion but only a 5.3 in the Thin-Ice Skating."

"What are you, kidding? Did you hear how he ducked out of that conversation about him running off with Celia in that Thunderbird! No, I gave him a 5.9, plus 5.6 for the Track. Mama, though, she gets a perfect 6.0 for the nagging."

Relatives with the highest score could win a special prize—perhaps a gold, silver, or bronze albatross in honor of the one they've inevitably hung around your neck. Best yet, not only do these Olympics give new meaning to the phrase "family fun," but you don't have to sit through tear-jerky bios about the participants because, hey, you've lived in them!

3. **If you're single, grab a buddy.** When I went to day camp as a little kid, we weren't allowed to go swimming unless we each had a buddy. The theory was that, even though the two of us could only doggie paddle, we'd somehow prevent each other from drowning by holding hands whenever the lifeguard blew his whistle.

The same theory might work with families. Make a pact with a friend to be each other's buddy. Go with your friend to her family's house for one holiday, then have her join you at yours the next.

Most families, no matter how pathological, try to behave themselves if they have "company." Going home with your friend for Thanksgiving will immediately force her relatives to be on their best behavior, while simultaneously absolving you of having to deal with yours. Then, when your buddy comes home with you for the winter holidays, her presence will force *your* family to be on their best behavior, while absolving her of having to deal with *hers*. Volley back and forth like this, and you could conceivably go for years without having to deal with your relatives in their pure, unadulterated state.

Of course, the minute your mother says to your buddy,

"Oh, just call me Mom. You're practically family now," the gig is up. But until then, you're helping to keep each other afloat, even if all you know how to do is the doggie paddle.

4. **Some people swap wives, so why not entire families?** Organize it like a Secret Santa. Get everybody who dreads going home to put their last name into a hat. Then, whichever family you draw, that's where you go for the holidays.

5. **Let's take a page from the family-values fanatics.** Every so often, when they're not busy terrorizing abortion clinics or parading in front of Planned Parenthood with giant plastic fetuses, the family-values fanatics lobby to pass "parental consent laws." These require teenage girls to get their parents' permission before obtaining an abortion. Funnily enough, backers of these laws rarely come out and say: "Hey, we're trying to pass these laws to curtail abortion." They don't even own up to the fact that maybe, just maybe, a few of them get a vengeful, puritanical thrill out of making life more difficult for sexually active girls. Oh, no. These folks insist that passing consent laws will make families closer by "compelling teenagers to talk to their parents."

Now, of course, anyone who thinks you can make a teenager talk to her parents by passing legislation (a) has obviously never *been* a teenager, (b) has obviously never *had* a teenager, and (c) is a total fucking moron.

And yet, the far right continually insists on trying to change and shape fundamental human relationships through legislation and doctrine. There are the Baptists, deciding in prehistoric 1998 that all women should "submit" to their husbands as decreed in the Bible. There are some right-to-lifers who believe that women should not be able to get an abortion without the consent of their husbands. Conservatives are constantly talking about laws that will "reinstate morality," "strengthen the family," and "restore the family." (And they actually do this with a *straight face.* I mean, at least the British Members of Parliament who advocate family values often have the good taste to get caught attempting autoerotic asphyxiation with "young rent boys" in high heels and garters.)

But recently I got to thinking: Maybe the Christian Coalition and their buddies have a point. Maybe the legal system *really* is the best way to try and change family dynamics. Hell, nothing else seems to work. Who's to say that using laws to govern intimacy is really that stupid after all?

The problem with the family-values zealots may not be that they're trying to legislate family values—it may be that they're simply trying to legislate the wrong ones.

I mean, if you really want women to be more devoted to their families, try passing the following laws instead:

- No phone calls from relatives asking if we've met "anybody nice" yet.

- Parents are prohibited from asking, "So when are you going to get a life already?" "Why don't you fix yourself up a little?" and "Are you sure you want to eat that?" Ditto for inquiring about our friends' marital status, mentioning our biological clock, or critiquing the way we raise our kids.

- If we're gay, family members cannot keep checking to see if we've "changed our mind" yet.

- The following discussions are permanently banned from all family reunions:

  Our weight.

  Our love lives.

  Comparisons of our salary, looks, and education with those of our siblings, step-siblings, and/or cousins.

  Why we didn't go out on a second date with that lovely dental hygienist our cousin Alma set us up with.

- If uncles, brothers, fathers, nephews, and so forth, pinch us on the ass, make a pass at us, or utter inappropriate sexual comments, we have a legal right to clobber them.

- Parents and other relations must not play favorites.

- No karaoke machines.

And if they don't adhere to these laws?
I say: Sue.

Part III

❦

Ruling
the World

Chapter 16

꩜

Everything We Need to Know
We Learn from Shopping

Nothing cheers a girl up like shopping.

—MADONNA

When I worked at *Glamour* magazine one summer during college, it fell to me to do the incredibly glamourous job of opening the mail.

Earlier that year, in one of its reader questionnaires, *Glamour* had asked women if they were "shop-a-holics." As I began sorting through the responses, it became clear to me that I'd stumbled upon a twelve-step program that was so anonymous, its own members didn't even know they were in it.

Hundreds upon hundreds of women, of all ages and backgrounds, confessed to being compulsive shoppers. They wrote in great, lurid detail about the extreme pleasure they got from shopping. For some, it was a matter of "just looking"; others had developed a dangerous habit of grandiose "impulse" buying. But whatever their version of the vice, these gals wrote with fervency and passion, with lots of exclamation points and triple-underlined words, describing how they literally got high at the mall: "After I make a purchase, I feel exhilarated," one woman wrote. "I can't wait to get home and look at it. I have a buzz for the rest of the day."

"Every night, on my way home from work, I just have to swing by the stores for one quick fix," wrote another.

Mind you, these were not rich girls. Some were living so far beyond their means, they'd had to file for bankruptcy or landed in Debtors Anonymous. And yet they continued to, ahem, charge ahead.

Why?

Woman after woman said that shopping gave her a sense of "power" and "control." In fact, *power* and *control* appeared so frequently in the letters, they started to sound like a theme song or a mantra.

"People *wait* on me," one woman wrote proudly. "I feel such *power.*"

"When I'm shopping, I'm able to get exactly what I *want,*" explained another. "I'm totally in *control.*"

For many of us, sadly, a store is the only female-centered domain where we feel we have total veto power and the ability to pick and choose as we like. Jobs, families, and relationships, of course, require constant and often unequal compromises. Even Temples of Girliness, like salons, have a degree of surrender involved: Once we're in the swivel chair and the bib, hey, we're at the mercy of the stylist. In a spa, we're wrapped in a towel and led around like a baby, vulnerable and naked, hoping the masseuse isn't a sadist. And the gynecologist? Don't get us started.

But in a store: Hel-lo! We are suddenly duchesses with dollars, queens with cash, prima donnas with plastic. Provided a boutique isn't too snooty or racist, we are utterly transformed beneath those fabulous fluorescent lights. We preside over endless possibilities, over aisles full of new delicious goodies to admire and possess. Even if we're flat broke, we can indulge our fantasies, imagining ourselves remade, our homes redecorated, our wardrobes revamped.

And so, at a time when women are overwhelmed with choices and conflicting desires, why not approach our entire lives like K-Mart or Nordstrom?

Okay, I admit it sounds fatuous. But think about it. Even if we hate buying clothes—even if we get a mall headache just looking at a catalog—even if we think capitalism is the root of all evil—we girls *know* how to shop. As soon as we're old enough to point and say, "I want," our culture grooms us for shopping, breeds us for shopping, coaches us in shopping: Every magazine, TV show, movie, and advertisement is dedicated to cultivating us as conspicuous consumers, to getting us salivating over stuff and spending our shekels. In America, Gettin' the Goods has been elevated to a sport—not to mention a religion, an art form, and a talent. It's a wonder stores don't hold a Shopping Olympics—with competitions in, say, Bargain Hunting and the Fifty-Yard Dash to the Cash Register.

Yet, at the same time, so many of us gals are besieged with life decisions: We don't know whether to downsize or supersize our careers, whom to commit to romantically, where to live, how to live, if and when to have kids. It's like we're faced with a buffet table of opportunities but can only go through the serving line once. Many of us don't know where the hell to start. Or what to choose. Or how to balance the main course with everything else we want on our plates. We've seen the Baby Boomers ahead of us at the table, piling everything on at once. And we've seen them get sick and exhausted and lose their appetites in the process.

We ask ourselves: Can we, in fact, have it all? How do we make smart choices? What do we even *want*? We're constantly second-guessing our priorities.

But give us two hours at Macy's, and hel-lo.

Suddenly, we're Madonna.

Set us loose in a storewide sale, and we're instantly transformed into ambitious material girls who know exactly what we want and how to get it. Whether our fetish is shoes, books, or power tools, we're unabashed in our desires. Out of our way, please. Those black-velvet dress pants have *our* name on them. Could we see the silver bracelets instead of the gold? And make that a *double* skim latté, no whip.

We're actually *emboldened* by the possibilities before us. We take delight in picking and choosing, in sorting through the racks and bins. Sometimes, in fact, going into a store *without* a clue is the most fun of all. Project! Challenge! Treasure hunt!

In a store, we know how to study our options, assess our budget, and make authoritative decisions.

In a store, we can discern what's of lasting quality and what's not, what's worth our money and what's not, and what's worth waiting in line for—and what's not.

In a store, we don't hesitate to ask for help to get what we want.

We know a good deal when we see one.

And we know how to drive a hard bargain, need be.

So why not apply these skills to our lives *beyond* the cash register? I mean, not to put too fine a point on it, but wouldn't it benefit us occasionally if we could treat our bosses and lovers like salesclerks? After all, we never have trouble telling some guy at Valu Village exactly what we need.

Or consider this: One of my friends plans when she's going to shop based on the big annual sales. She waits to get a raincoat during President's Day, hits the factory outlets on vacation, and goes to the mall the day after Christmas to stock up on wrapping paper for the next December. She even follows a formula called CPW (cost per wear) that she read about in *Self* magazine, so she can make sure that each time she's going to shell out big Bennies for a major clothing purchase, she'll really be getting her money's worth. Three hundred dollars for a skirt, she reasons, comes down to less than a dollar a day.

But ask her where she sees herself professionally in a year, and she says, "Oh, gosh, I don't know. How can you plan a career?"

Or there's my friend Andrea, who's an expert at shopping for cars. She knows how to do her homework, walk into a dealership, shmooze the salesguy, and stand her ground until she gets the model she wants for the price she wants. But she's loath to ask for a raise at her job. "I have more trouble assessing and asking for my own financial worth than for that of a Honda," she admits.

And as for all those shop-a-holics and credit-card junkies out there: Studies have shown that women are better than men at picking stocks and managing mutual funds precisely because we've been raised to be savvy shoppers. So why not harness these skills to work *in reverse* for us financially?

"Wall Street is the ultimate shopping mall," said a binge shopper I know. "Whenever I get the urge to splurge, I invest the money instead. I get the same thrill buying a couple of shares of stock as I do buying nail polish." In both instances, she says, she gets to shop around and find out what's hot: "But when I purchase a couple of shares of stock, there's an added kick to it because I actually stand to make money on what I've just bought."

(Funny, but we gals know that you don't have to be rich to enjoy yourself at the mall but, like most Americans, we tend to believe that you either have to be rich or a slightly psychotic e-trader to own stocks. Not so. It is possible to make something out of nearly nothing. National Public Radio reported that if you take the price of a pair of new shoes—say, seventy-five dollars—and sock it away at eight-percent interest in a no-load mutual fund, it'll be worth four thousand dollars in fifty years. Not bad when you consider that the shoes themselves probably won't make it past next season.)

And since most of us would like to shop till we drop with someone special in tow, why not give our prospective lovers as much consideration as we give, say, a dress?

After all, if we have to buy a pricey outfit for a wedding, it's usually a major undertaking. We'll even "prep" for it: scouring the stores, maybe checking out newspaper ads and magazines. And we *know* the rules: Rarely will we buy the first dress we try on, even if it looks stunning on us. Oh, no. We'll have to try on at least two dozen others to make sure the first really is the best. Then we'll drag our girls in to look at it. We'll mentally go through our closets to make sure it works with the other things in our wardrobe. We'll ask ourselves: Does this really suit me? Is it flattering? Can I move and breathe in it? Does it have to be dry-cleaned? Will it break my bank? Will I wear it only once—or will I use it again?

The purchase becomes an item of existential import and consideration.

But let some hottie at the cash register ask us out, and we'll write our phone number on the back of a gum wrapper without a second thought. Our clothes we treat like investments, but our dates? Impulse purchases.

If we gals want some high-quality, durable goods in the romance department, I say we've got to remember that *nothing* we pick up on a whim on the check-out line is usually anything we want hanging around our house two years later. And we shouldn't grab the first person who seems halfway decent, either. We've got to do a little comparison shopping—and ask ourselves: Does this person really suit me? Do they give me room to move and breathe? Are they easy to care for? Will they break my bank? And really: Are they good for more than one night?

(Because, face it: It's one thing to want a Versace gown or an Armani tuxedo. It's another to actually have to wear it 24/7.)

Plus, as with any shopping spree, we've got to be open to those offbeat possibilities, to the orange feather boa that actually looks fabulous with the old brown jacket.

"Love is like shopping," says my friend Suzy, who's developed elaborate theories about the subject. "It's like if you have to buy a dress for a fancy party. You usually look for something slinky and black, because that's what you're expected to wear, right? But then, as you're browsing, maybe you'll see this pink angora sweater on the sale rack. It's not what you're looking for, but you figure, 'What the hell, I'll try it on.' And it looks great, so you buy it.

"Well, by the time the party rolls around, you still haven't found a slinky black dress. So you wear the pink sweater. You dress it up with a string of pearls, and it's just fine. In fact, you feel more comfortable and special in that sweater than you would in some tight black number. And soon that pink sweater becomes your favorite thing in your closet. You can dress it up, dress it down, and you always feel good in it. Maybe your mother will say to you, '*That's* what you're wearing?' But so what. It's what's best for you."

Well, the same holds true for finding a partner, she says. Sure, we may think a slinky black dress is our best bet. But the truth of the matter is, we may get far more mileage—and happiness—out of a fuzzy pink sweater.

So enough with those shopworn feminist theories that claim women will acquire power by acting like men. Enough with those passé assertions that women will acquire power by acting like earth mothers or sex goddesses. The real deal is this: Women will acquire power by acting like *shoppers*. Whether we're dealing with our careers, our fortunes, or our love lives, I'm telling you: Live like a bargain hunter, rule like an Amazon.

Chapter 17

ᕲᕫ

Career Advice and Nail Polish

*If women can sleep their way to
the top, how come they aren't there?
There must be an epidemic of
insomnia out there.*
—ELLEN GOODMAN

Last year I got a call from my very hip younger cousin, Gail, out in San Francisco. She's the co-director of a pilot program for the homeless.

"I need some smart career advice, Cuz," she said. (Yeah, we really do call each other "Cuz." We're dorks.) "I'm meeting with the mayor's office tomorrow to see about securing an eighty-thousand-dollar grant for our program and, well, I'm just not sure about something—"

"What's the problem?" I asked.

"Well, do I remove my blue nail polish, or can I keep it on?"

"This is the career advice you want?" I said.

"Well, what else am I supposed to ask?" she said.

Zoiks. These days, sound career advice for young women is harder to come by than a bra that actually fits. Ironically, while we females are constantly bombarded with pointers on stuff like how to give a blow job or get rock-hard abs just like Gwyneth's ("Just do six hundred stomach crunches a day! Weigh down your feet with cans of cling peaches!"), real Working Girl wisdom is so rare, some of us don't even know what it looks like.

Yeah, there are the inevitably pedantic relatives offering such gems as: "I'm telling you, learn data processing. Any idiot can do it." (Meanwhile their kids are still programming their VCRs for them.)

There are career counselors who, by virtue of the fact that they themselves have made a career out of *career counseling*, inspire Zero confidence whatsoever.

And then there are the "career" pages in women's magazines—which are terribly helpful if you want to know whether it's okay to have sex with a co-worker on top of the photocopier.

On some level, it's as if our culture sill regards women's careers as hobbies—as slightly narcissistic diversions that we chicks take up in vain attempts to be "just like men" or to shirk our responsibilities as mothers. Some people are still giving lip service to that demented Harvard study from over a decade ago that erroneously said women over thirty-five were more likely to be killed by terrorists than to get married ("Like there's a difference?" says one married friend). But they've conveniently developed amnesia about the study released in the late nineties that found career women are often more fulfilled than homemakers—and that their kids benefit from this. It's as if the culture still refuses to take us seriously, as if it's saying subconsciously, "For God's sake, let's not encourage the broads!"

Plus, unfortunately, careers are one area in which being a blue nail polish–wearing, fabulously tatooed, beautifully attitudinal SmartMouth Goddess is not automatically self-empowering. To the majority of bosses, "attitude" is something that usually goes hand in hand with the word *problem*.

So, if you're a righteous babe just starting out on a career path, how might you navigate the terrain?

Since my friends and I have finally moved beyond entry-level positions, allow us to share some words of wisdom, straight from the cubicles, copiers, and corporate boardrooms . . .

- **First and foremost, remember: The twenties basically suck.** Lots of people will tell you that the twenties are the best years of your life. Do not believe them. They are either sadists or morons.

  The early twenties can be a real shocker, especially if you've been in school all your life. All the prescriptive ground rules of high school and college that everyone spent years bitching about are suddenly gone, leaving you in free-fall. Suddenly, just when you're legally old enough to drink, you have to pay rent and taxes. Student loans come due. You're no longer surrounded by cohorts who are happy to stay up until 4:00 A.M. discussing Alice Walker and drinking Jell-O shots. The Big Three L's of adulthood—labor, love, and location—loom as a giant question mark.

  If you're gay, you've got to deal with whether to come out to a whole new set of questionably intelligent and questionably progressive people. If you're straight, suddenly everyone's trying to fix you up with their dumb-ass nephew and telling you that if you don't hurry up and settle down, you'll be bitter and lonely by the time you're thirty.

  In the middle of all of this, you're expected to map out your future.

  Is it any wonder that people in their twenties often have nervous breakdowns, develop hypochondria, get married too young to the wrong people, or voluntarily apply for inter-minable Ph.D. programs?

  Look, since your twenties are basically going to be chaos anyway, do as my grandma said to do: Take advantage of them and use the time to get some real life experiences. Travel, if you can. Try a new city. Suffer through a bunch of humiliating entry-level positions in the name of "comparison shopping."

  Waitress in a scummy bar while you take voice lessons during the day or pursue your painting. Work for noble causes and nonprofits you believe in; chances are, like most do-gooder organizations, they'll pay you crap, treat you like shit, and work you to death, but hey! It beats becoming a corporate weenie at twenty-three and working eighty-hour weeks for some crypto-fascist corporation that leaves you with zilch for a soul.

Now is the time when you can afford to experiment. For never again will you think it's kind of groovy to share an apartment with two other girls in the meat-packing district and eat dinner every night at bars that serve free ravioli and nachos during happy hour.

- **At the same time, don't be an idiot.** Being a ballerina is not a viable career if you have enormous breasts. The rent does have to be paid. It wouldn't kill you to waitress.

- **Watch out for law school.** Be forewarned: Go to law school without a passion for it and prepare to have a midlife crisis by age thirty. The most professionally miserable people I know are lawyers who went to law school because they had delusions of "security" and didn't know what the hell else to do. Sure, you can always "do something" with a law degree. Like hang it on your wall while you go to work for a Web-design firm, run for Congress, or move to Berkeley to practice colonic irrigation (similar to law, actually).

- **Watch out for Ph.D. programs in the liberal arts.** Unless you are truly dying for a career in academia—that is, if you love to teach and research using phrases like "postmodernist deconstructive valuations of the neocolonial hierarchy" and get paid thirty-two thousand a year to use them in places like Toadsuck, Arkansas (I'm not making that up)—do not, under any circumstance, go to Ph.D. programs in the liberal arts.

- **Treat a career like a lover.** Ideally, a career should get you hot and bothered. Why commit to doing something you hate? Like a marriage, it won't last if you're miserable. If you had a lover who lay around the house for years doing nothing but watching *Star Trek* reruns and drinking Mountain Dew, draining you of precious time and energy, you'd haul his sorry ass to the curb. Well, ditto for any job like that.

- **At the same time, stop whining. Everyone has to start somewhere.** Recently, I met an eighteen-year-old girl who'd gotten a plum internship with the State Department. "It's okay for now," she informed me, "but I don't want to work there. I mean, I don't want some entry-level job or something."

  Or *something*? Honey, I wanted to say: you're *eighteen*. What do you think they should hire you as—the ambassador to Burkina Faso?

  Entry-level positions are crummy but inevitable. Most employers know that you only need the IQ of soap to make copies and change the toner cartridge. Although some will hire you because they actually derive pleasure from insulting your intelligence, others actually hire you with an eye toward grooming you for bigger and better things, provided you prove your mettle.

  Either way, there's stuff to be learned by paying your dues. Arrogance, however, is not one of them. Sure, you might be able to design a Web site or make foreign policy better than the twits upstairs, but employers want to make sure you're a known quantity and a "team player" before they hand you the keys to the company Cadillac or set you up in your own embassy.

- **Overnight sensations have a terrible track record.** Don't beat yourself up if you're not a wunderkind. Everybody hates a prodigy. Unless you're an athlete, actress, or physicist, you'll actually do better in your field if you're *not* stratospherically successful by age twenty-seven. If you reach your peak early on, where is there to go but down? Better to be like a fine wine than a flavor-of-the-month.

- **Connections, connections, connections.** Getting a job is rarely based on pure merit alone. Equally important, sometimes, is "who you know and who you blow," as my dad once so delicately put it. The privileged dipshits who oppose affirmative action conveniently overlook this.

Case in point: One year, I taught writing at the University of Michigan. During a class discussion, a bunch of guys (all wealthy, white eighteen-year-olds: big surprise) complained to me about the "reverse discrimination" of affirmative action. So I asked students to go around the room and list every job they had ever worked and how they'd gotten it. Out of approximately one hundred students, ninety-eight percent had gotten their jobs through their school or someone they knew—whether they were scooping ice cream or interning at a white-glove law firm.

Such cronyism would be a dirty little secret of the American meritocracy, except that we practice it very openly, aggressively, and proudly through assorted networking parties, alumni functions, and professional associations. It's common knowledge that, if you're looking for a job, the first thing you should do is get on the horn and contact every single person you've so much as blinked at.

Similarly, when people look to hire someone, they tend to go to the wells that are most familiar to them: alumni associations, sororities and fraternities, professional organizations, social clubs, and friends. And professionals know this. Which is why they play golf and care about sending their kids to Dartmouth instead of community college. And which is why, incidently, all the people who argue that affirmative action is discriminatory, and "true merit" is all you need, are clearly full of shit. They have got to know that if someone helps open a door for you, frankly, it's easier to get your foot in.

So don't expect that a degree, an experience, or a great job evaluation alone will necessarily take you where you want to go. Whether you're looking for your first job or your fifth, get on the phone and work it, Girls. Don't be shy: Call everyone you know—friends, alums, former employers. Tell 'em you're looking. Ask them whom they'd recommend to do an informational interview with you. Network like maniacs. Since women are accused of being talkaholics anyway, use it to your advantage. Consider it your own little form of self-affirmative action. Really, it pays to be brazen.

- **Assess, then impress.** This is the hardest lesson my friends and I have had to learn starting out in a new job. Luckily, another woman who's also had problems with it is Hillary Clinton.

  When Hillary came to Washington as the First Lady way back in 1993, she didn't bother to learn the lay of the land. She dove headlong into overhauling the national health-care system, oblivious to the work environment and politics around her. As a result, she might as well have done a swan dive off an overpass.

  Sometimes, we gals feel we have to prove ourselves twice as much as the boys. We come into a new job like gangbusters, without taking the time to develop an understanding of the office culture. And so our good intentions boomerang. People experience us as loose cannons and mavericks.

  Sometimes it's better to hang back for a little while, size up your new situation, and then turn up your wattage full blast. Because remember: When someone new comes on board, people don't worry that she's incompetent nearly so much as they worry she'll step on their turf and hog the good stapler.

- **You may be able to have it all. You just might not be able to have it all at once.** Most of us fabulous femmes do not parlay our own hip-hop record label into a multimillion-dollar empire while cooking for our own restaurant, designing our own Chinese silk handbags, managing a stock portfolio, teaching scuba to underprivileged children, traveling with our anthropologist husband to Togo, and home schooling four exquisite kids in a house that would make Martha Stewart or B. Smith cream.

  Like supermodels, the three working women in the world who may actually have achieved this are freaks of nature. And like supermodels, they have a lot of people behind the scenes working to help them succeed. Instead of personal trainers, stylists, and dieticians, they have personal assistants, nannies, and servants. Trying to be just like them will only make you insane.

- **Finally, if you do have to ask some bigwig for money, remove the blue nail polish.** Ditto for the tongue rings, miniskirts, and body glitter. Your older sisters know these things are the bomb, but chances are it may remind many power brokers of the drunken teenagers who once drove a dune buggy through the plate-glass window of their vacation home. Play it cool by playing it down.

Chapter 18

☙☙

Never Mind a Penis,
We'll Take a Bigger Paycheck

I've been rich and I've been poor.
Rich is better.

—Sophie Tucker

Recently, a young feminist headmistress of a prestigious private school confessed to me that she pays her male teachers more than her female teachers. Why?

"Because the men *ask*," she said. "They negotiate their salaries better and demand more money than the women do. They also lobby for raises, which the women don't."

Uh-oh.

Soon after this conversation, I attended an annual women's networking dinner in Washington, DC. When I repeated this story, the room fell silent for a moment as a wave of self-recognition swept over the guests. Some were power brokers, others were wannabes. But their reactions were the same.

"Oh, my God. I am terrible about negotiating my own money!" said a woman who heads a multimillion-dollar foundation. "Every time I've been asked to name my salary, I've completely low-balled myself."

A woman who'd spent years as a foreign bureau chief for the *Washington Post* confessed, "As a journalist, I can ask Idi Amin about terrorism or Saddam Hussein about the Kurds. But ask my boss for a raise? Forget it."

"Anytime I walk into a job interview and they tell me what the position pays, I just feel grateful that they want to hire me," admitted a cable-television producer.

No wonder we gals are the cheapest dates on the job market! Certainly, employers get us at a bargain. And while the inferior size of our paychecks isn't our fault (thank you, patriarchy), our please-kind-Sir-might-I-have-a-bit-more-gruel attitude ain't exactly helping, either.

"Women always undersell themselves. It almost seems like a biological imperative," my own boss, Kate, has observed.

Of course, this is no big surprise. Traditionally, money has "happened" to women. And despite feminism, many of us have gotten a lot of old-fashioned ideas about money almost by osmosis: A lot of gals still believe on some level that wealth is a "guy thing"; that guys are threatened by women who earn big bucks; and that, ultimately, a man should "take care" of us.

It's no wonder that women are the fastest-growing group of gamblers in America! We have a long history of investing in fairy tales and having our fortunes determined by luck.

Ironically, in a culture where it's No Big Deal to tell TV audiences about a threesome we had with our best friend and her stepbrother, discussing money is still curiously taboo. The Great Green Goddess today is like what sex was back in the 1950s; plenty of gals are gettin' it, but nobody's talking. It occurs to me that over the years my friends and I have taught each other how to use tampons, how to give a blow job, how to put a condom on a guy using our mouth, and so forth. But how to manage money? The topic has almost never come up. You'd think we were all heiresses who didn't have to worry—you know, heiresses who just happened to *like* working at Kinko's.

If we ask older, well-heeled women about money, they often look at us as if they've just smelled a fart. *Darling*, they say, *that's tacky.*

The only female financial "role models" many of us have been exposed to on a regular basis are: (1) celebrities who pull down enormous paychecks and buy million-dollar digs in Beverly Hills while wearing three thousand dollars' worth of Prada and holding a Chihuahua, (2) struggling single mothers paying for Mac 'n' cheese with their laundry quarters, or (3) Betty and Wilma, running through the stores of Bedrock with Fred and Barney's credit cards, shouting, "Charge it!"

How delightfully, er, Stone Age.

It doesn't help either that, in the past, feminists condemned capitalism as patriarchal and exploitive. Yeah, well. Whatever. These women obviously never tried to buy tampons in Communist China in 1986.

Money is a power tool, and we material girls know it. Even *Ms.* magazine has finally learned that it's great to have some Sugar Mommies around: Recently, the magazine almost folded until it was rescued by a band of wealthy women. So Gloria and the gang can tell us: If girls are rich enough to pick up our own tab, we don't have to be beholden to anyone—be they men or corporate advertisers who want us to pimp feminine deodorant spray on our editorial pages.

How do we learn to bring home the big bucks, plump our portfolios, and foster a sense of entitlement? How do we transform ourselves from the Divas of Diddly into the High Priestesses of Higher Pay? From Minimum-Wage Mamas into Matriarchs of Moolah?

Well, for starters, we've got to cash in any outmoded attitudes we may have about money and gender. Poverty ain't pink, and greenbacks ain't blue. There's nothing feminine about being scatterbrained about money, and there's nothing masculine about earning it. This sounds silly and patronizing (excuse me, matronizing) in print, but as Lillian Vernon, the CEO of her own corporation, once observed, "The one thing I think women sometimes have a real problem with is making money. They consider that unfeminine."

Yeah, well, there's unfeminine, and then there's unconscious. Any woman living on welfare, trapped in a trailer park, or eking out an existence on Social Security will agree: There is no feminine glory in not being able to create options for ourselves.

Besides, it's one thing to want a guy who's financially capable of standing on his own two feet. Nobody wants to date a barnacle. But it's another to expect men to support us financially till death do us part. This isn't a matter of feminism but realism: There are all sorts of curveballs awaiting us in life. And like good Girl Scouts, we've got to be prepared. Even squirrels have a backup plan.

Besides, if a *guy* is threatened because we earn good money (as if!), then he's clearly impoverished in the ego department. It's not our job to build up his self-worth by diminishing our net worth. And though guys are supposedly threatened by babes who earn bucks, they have utter *contempt* for those who don't. Just look at how this nation treats women on welfare.

But along with changing our minds, we divas also have to resist the desire to buy all of our fantasies.

Let's not be fooled by the cool shit so many people seem to own: the Nokia cell phones, Gucci shoes, and sport utility vehicles driven by yuppies in loafers who've never taken an unbeaten path in their life. Our economy is dedicated to selling us all kinds of nonessential crappola, and most Americans today live beyond their means and are mired in credit-card debt. Problem is, while their purchases are readily visible, their abysmal credit reports are not. Credit cards are aptly called *plastic* because, just like plastic surgery, they create the illusion that people are better off than they really are. They put an artificial face, a "lift," on people's appearances.

Plus, for too many of us, VISA is a sugar daddy, always there to buy us stuff when the whim hits. I say, let's cut the cord and cut up the cards if we can't live within our means. No way should those giant corporate patriarchs like Citibank or First National make nineteen-and-a-half-percent interest off us each month. Credit cards are vampires. Let 'em sink their fangs into our neck and we won't pay them off until we reach menopause.

Instead of subjecting ourselves to such monthly financial bloodletting, I think we should develop some big fat assets for the world to kiss instead.

Usually, when we girls are taught about risk, it's framed in terms of what we shouldn't do—like have unprotected sex or wear a black bra under a white shirt to a water park. We're not educated about taking financial risks that might have big payoffs.

But playing the stock market is a far smarter way for righteous babes to take a few gambles. Time to put our common sense into common stocks and give the good ol' boys at Merrill Lynch a run for their money. Hell, if we can watch our weight, we can follow Wall Street. It's all about gains, losses, and anticipated growth.

Plus, in the past few years a whole spate of books has been written to help us gals get a financial life and invest. There's also plenty of stuff online. Better still, for those of us who want to be Capitalists with a Conscience, there are a range of socially responsible, environmentally friendly, tobacco-free, pro-women mutual funds out there. So we can reap some dividends without pawning our principles.

But ultimately, if we gals really want more coinage in our coffers, the bottom line is that we've got to make like the boys and *ask* for it.

Obviously, this is far easier said than done.

So often, our desire to be liked overshadows our ability to negotiate a salary. We worry that if we ask for more money, we'll alienate our employers and scuttle the deal. Other times, we want to be hired and accepted so much, we don't pay proper attention to the bucks. A job offer instantly transforms us into Sally Field: "You like me! You really like me!" we shout, so pleased to receive the stamp of approval that our employers could probably hand us a fake gold statuette as payment and we'd feel lucky.

A few years ago, I was offered a prestigious job for a nonprofit that asked me to "name" my price. When I consulted friends and colleagues about how to proceed, the advice I received was so cleanly divided along gender lines, you'd think it had been imported from Mars and Venus respectively.

The guys immediately geared up for hardball. "Sixty thousand bucks," they told me, their voices like gavels. "Not a penny less. Start with seventy. Let 'em bargain you down. If they don't give you sixty thousand, walk. Better yet, get a counteroffer from another agency first, then squeeze 'em by the balls."

But the gals? "Well, it *is* a nonprofit," they invariably began, their voices hesitant and lilting, all chamomile and conciliation. "So you don't want to ask for too much, I guess. I dunno, maybe thirty-five thousand? After all, it's not like your boss has an unlimited budget, and you *do* want her to hire you . . ."

For the guys, salary negotiations are about, well, salary. The bottom line is the bottom line. But for the girls? Salary negotiations are about *negotiation*. They're about weighing our employer's needs and showing the boss we're a "team player" who's "considerate" by not being too demanding in the Dollar Department. *If we want too much,* our thinking goes, *people might not want us.*

"Women approach negotiations emotionally rather than as business," says my friend Jennifer, who's been president of her own company. "I see it time and time again."

Part of the problem is that salary negotiations are combative: "They're about battle and strategy," says my friend Desa, who regularly negotiates for money. "These things we're not traditionally schooled in."

Ain't that the truth. The only strategies we gals seem to get traditionally schooled in (ad nauseam, I might add) are "man-catching" tactics. Time and time again, we're inundated with advice on how to "hook" a guy, attract love, and "make him want you." *Don't give it away, girls,* we're chronically told. *He won't pay the cow if she gives milk for free.*

Yet when it comes to salary negotiations, most of us are given zero guidance whatsoever. So we give our milk away for free in the workplace all the time. Great.

But it occurs to me that we could use this irony to our advantage. Why not take all that frilly sex-and-relationship advice—all those "time-tested secrets" for capturing the heart of Mr. Right—and apply them to salary negotiations instead?

For example, one of the oldest lines of dating advice is: *You can't find true love until you love yourself first.* Well, before we seek a better salary, we've got to "love ourselves," too. We've gotta believe that we're valuable in the marketplace, that we deserve big Bennies, and that we're entitled to ask for them. Just like in relationships, a sense of self-worth is a prerequisite to getting what we want.

We're also told: *Be really clear about what you're looking for in a man. Make a list and stick to it.* Well, before we demand anything in salary negotiations, we've got to figure out what *we* want, what we *need* to live on, and what's the lowest price we can realistically settle for—and stick to it, too.

This way, in addition to serving as nifty doorstops and hot plates, books like *The Rules* or *Guerrilla Dating Tactics* can actually do us some good. So many reactionary prescriptions for "Getting the Guy" that we learn from self-help gurus, relatives, and women's magazines are far better suited to the negotiating table—where they don't smack of emotional trickery and can make us the mistresses of our own fortune, instead of *man*-ipulators.

Here's how some classic "man-catching" tactics might actually help make *us* the millionaires we're supposedly dying to marry.

- *Act aloof and mysterious. Don't talk too much.* Studies show that job candidates routinely ask for less money than employers are prepared to pay—and women tend to ask for less than men. So when it comes to salary negotiations, it literally pays for us to hold back and keep our mouths shut. We shouldn't broach the subject of money; let the employer bring it up first. And then, let the employer name a salary first, too. After all, once a gal names her price, the negotiations can only go down from there.

- *Let the man make the first move.* If an employer asks what kind of salary we're looking for, never say, "I need at least *X* amount of money." Don't let them know what you'll settle for, either. Instead, try to make them make the first move and name a number, even if you have to do this by responding to their question with another question: "What does the position pay?" or "What is your range?"

If the employer claims not to know what the position pays (yeah, right), suggest they get back to you when they do.

If they say, "Tell us what you want," name a salary that's so astronomically high, they laugh or gasp. Then you can say, "Well, okay, if a million dollars isn't in your ball park, what is?" (Interesting note: I did this several times, and it worked like a charm. I got a laugh *and* a clue. Another friend of mine did this once—she asked for twenty thousand dollars more than the position was supposed to pay—and the company gave it to her.)

If the employer names a number lower than you want, say, "Well, I'm really looking for—" and name the top end of your range plus ten to twenty percent. If they respond with, "We can't afford that," ask them what they can.

In order for this to work, of course, we've got to have done our homework beforehand. In addition to keeping in mind the amount that *we* want, we should know in advance what a particular job tends to pay, including those that pay by the hour (just fifty-cents-an-hour more means an extra thousand dollars in a year of forty-hour workweeks). This way, we know what to expect, and what sum is realistic to aim for. We should also bear in mind that entry-level salaries are far less negotiable than those of mid- and upper-level positions. The lower we are on the ladder, the less leeway we have.

Luckily, since Americans always want to know who's got the proverbial bigger dick, researching salaries is not too difficult. We can check trade-association newspapers, financial magazines, surf the Net, and ask other people in the profession. Calling employment agencies and checking salaries in the help-wanted ads helps, too. With a little Nancy Drewing, we'll be able to walk into a negotiation knowing Which Way Is Up.

• *Play hard-to-get.* Don't accept the very first offer. Test the waters instead. After an employer names the salary, say, "Well, I was actually hoping for more."

If they refuse to budge on the money, my friend Sarah (another career diva) suggests negotiating benefits, vacation days, profit sharing, and stock options. You also might ask: When will you be up for a salary review? How often might you expect a promotion? And get everything in writing.

Remember: It doesn't hurt to try. The worst they can say is no.

- *The man should pay for you on a date. Don't go dutch.* Because the person involved in salary negotiations is going to be our future employer, we often feel the impulse to prove that we're a helpful and cooperative future employee, that we're accommodating and willing to compromise easily. Meet them halfway? Sure, why not?

  But, remember, it's *our* salary that's on the line here. And each time we accept a job, our pay becomes part of our salary history—which is often used to calibrate salaries when we accept new positions in the future. (Job interviewers have an annoying habit of asking, "And how much are you earning at your present position?" Apparently, they can check, too, which makes bald-face lying tempting but not an option.) Therefore, what we negotiate now can affect what we negotiate at our next job as well. Plus, our salary also determines our Social Security, 401(k) plans, and pensions, if we get them.

  So, whenever possible, we've got to stand firm and make sure the company pays us decently and competitively. For when all the negotiating is said and done, we'll be living with our paychecks far longer than our bosses will be living with the memory of how "nice" or "flexible" we were during salary talks.

  Besides, *companies hate hiring as much as singles hate dating.* It's a grueling, boring process that takes the bigwigs away from what they really want to be doing: playing computer games and eating lunch. So if they find a job candidate they like, they really want to clinch the deal and be done with it. This works in our favor. They won't scuttle everything if we ask for an extra three grand. Again, the worst they can say is no.

- *If a man won't commit to you/give you a ring/treat you like a princess, leave him.* Part of negotiating means that we've got to be willing to walk if we're not treated (i.e., paid) respectably. "Remember, a job is like a relationship. If a relationship turns abusive, you've got to be able to leave. Well, if an employer doesn't want to pay you what you're worth, that's abusiveness, too," said Desa. "If you're not willing to walk away, then you relinquish your only source of power. You'll settle for anything, and so you'll get nothing."

- *Don't appear too eager with a man.* Finally: Try never, never to accept a salary offer on the spot. Even if they're offering you three million bucks and your own love-slave, reply, "Is that your final number? Okay, thank you. I'd like to think it over. I'll get back to you shortly."

   "Just like with sex, hold back a little. See if they'll sweeten the deal a little more to lure you in, whether it's with more money or benefits," says a corporate lawyer named LaTisha. "You don't want to appear too 'easy.' Just like guys don't value women they can hook up with real fast, companies tend to believe you're more valuable if you've been harder to get."

   Stupid, perhaps, but true.

   Of course, if we have trouble adopting these attitudes and making them second nature to us, I say we listen to the Liz Phair song "Shitloads of Money" over and over again. "It's nice to be liked," she croons, "but it's better by far to be paid."

   This tune should be our mantra—and the national anthem of the New Girl Order. Because we've got to remember: Being voted Miss Congeniality is all fine and dandy, but ultimately it won't earn us any power, it won't win us more respect—and certainly it won't pay the damn rent.

Cha-ching!

Chapter 19

ᛊ

Latifah Weapon, Brooklyn Porn

Whenever I see ads with the quote,
"You'll have to see this picture twice,"
I know it's the kind of picture
I don't want to see once.

—PAULINE KAEL

Why is it that Thelma and Louise, the only two chicks to have a truly excellent adventure in a big American movie, wound up driving off a cliff? Sure, it was a good film, but can't we also have some blockbusters where girls get to be romantic antiheroes and *not* commit suicide?

There are more women producers than ever working in Hollywood today, but you wouldn't know it going to the cineplex. Given the shallowness and limitations of most females in the movies, the movie theater is more like the "simplex." I mean, popcorn buckets have more depth than some of the stuff I've seen lately.

Back in the first half of the twentieth century, movie studios may have treated their stars like chattel, but they also had stars like

Bette Davis, Katharine Hepburn, and Elizabeth Taylor playing magnificent, juicy, complicated dames. In *All about Eve, Adam's Rib,* or *Who's Afraid of Virginia Woolf?* the main female characters are passionate and contradictory. Not a single one is a wisp in a slip dress.

Go to the movies today, and we basically see wisps in slip dresses playing one of the following:

A supposedly accomplished lawyer or detective who falls for a psycho-killer because, gosh, he's cute.

A waitress who falls for a racist obsessive-compulsive because, gosh, he's cute.

A US marshal who falls for a bank robber because, gosh, he's cute.

A woman with all the personality of a Nilla Wafer who begs her husband—the hero of the movie—to stop flying to the moon/fighting terrorists/tracking down JFK's assassins, so that he can stay home with her and the children.

A prostitute.

A girlfriend of a guy old enough to be her grandfather.

Part of a difficult mother-daughter relationship in which one of them is dying of cancer.

Chain-saw fodder.

Okay, maybe there are a few others, but *really*. Most gals in the movies rarely get to have fun: They're usually too busy being held hostage—in one way or another. Women have become such secondary, one-dimensional characters that any film that has more than one female in it is now instantly labeled a "chick flick." In fact, any film that doesn't blow up federal buildings and contain mind-numbing sequences of automatic-weapons fire is now considered a chick flick. I mean, *The Horse Whisperer* was called a chick flick, and it starred Robert Redford playing a cowboy.

Chick flick is also derogatory, the implication being, of course, that if it's designed to appeal to women, it's not worth seeing. Adding insult to injury: This is sometimes true. Some chick flicks really do suck. They're these insipid, refried fairy tales bathed in overdetermined sentimentality. But are they any worse than all those action movies with three hundred explosions and no coherent dialog? (Grunting is not dialog.) I don't *think* so.

Which is why I say we gals should start calling every big-screen bullet orgy a "dick flick" or "testicle fest." (Hey: If we're going to start sexual stereotyping and name-calling here, let's keep things equal, no? I mean: tit for tat, so to speak.) Next time a guy starts talking about how he wants to see *Lethal Weapon 30*, and not "some chick flick," just roll your eyes and go, "*Lethal Weapon 30*? Ugh. Testicle fest."

More and more, it seems popular media is becoming sexually stereotyped and segregated—on the small screen as well as the big. As I'm writing this, Fox Cable Network is launching The Boyz Channel and The Girlz Channel (so much for educational television—and they wonder why kids can't spell), separate channels with "gender-specific programming."

Then there's so-called reality television, which has elevated home movies and security-camera footage to an art form. We girls are being wooed with what the *Washington Post* dubbed "all-relationships-all-the-time." There's *A Wedding Story* and *Weddings of a Lifetime* (real! live! weepy! weddings!). *A Baby's Story* ("childbirth sagas") and *Reunion* (in which "long-lost relatives and friends fall tearfully into one another's arms").

Meanwhile, the guys get "shockumentary" shows like *Wildest Police Videos* (self-explanatory), *When Good Times Go Bad 2* (vacation disasters), *When Good Pets Go Bad* (psycho doggies), and *World's Most Shocking Medical Videos* (don't ask).

So, basically, we girls watch people get married, while boys watch them bungee jump into a caisson on their honeymoon. And this is how we're trained to see the world.

(Why not combine the two genres into *When Good Weddings Go Bad*? Now *that* would make for some interesting television that we'd *all* watch.)

In terms of the "fictional" TV shows, it doesn't get much better. There are now what? Over two hundred available channels, and yet almost none of them ever show women over 110 pounds or thirty-five years of age. In the movies it's even worse. Nowadays, actresses over twenty-five are considered "old."

None of this, unfortunately, is news. The question is, how can smart sisters deal with all this stupidity? I mean, it's one thing to be entertained; it's another to be insulted. And the line between the two is getting thinner than Calista Flockhart.

How do we generate alternative sources of entertainment and imagery—especially if we don't have access to our own movie studio or television production company? Or if we're among the 99.9 percent of the population that doesn't have the money to bankroll lots of nifty, pro-woman, multicultural HBO specials?

Well, it's not easy, but I say we resort to the first, last, and best source of entertainment available to all of us: our imaginations. And I say that we publicize whatever we dream up using our first, last, and best source of PR: our mouths.

This sounds like a stretch, but bear with me a moment.

All our "cultural traditions," all our fairy tales, adventure stories, and folklore, began with a bunch of bored, broke people sitting around making shit up. George Lucas and the late philosopher Joseph Campbell both claimed that the *Star Wars* series is a modern re-creation of such folklore. They even went so far as to say that *Star Wars* was a twentieth-century version of an "archetypal myth."

What makes a story an archetypal myth? Well, among other things, people sitting around telling it over and over for a zillion years. I mean, give an idea enough PR and eventually it takes on the sheen of universal truth.

So let's start talking, girls.

It's time to create some new archetypal myths. I'm sick of these "traditional stories" in which girls wait around semiconscious in some castle for a guy (or in the case of *Star Wars*, a guy and some robots) to rescue them. Frankly, we've come too far to live on in the cultural imagination as damsels in distress, hookers with hearts of gold, or policewomen in love with psychopaths. Nope. That shit is *old*, not *archetypal*, thank you. Time to claim some of the action, glory, and epic ambiguity for ourselves.

Look, to hear most of the stories handed down within our culture, you'd think that every guy from Odysseus onward was a knight, a maverick, an adventurer, a dreamer who dared to dream, a romantic outlaw, a brilliant inventor, or a conqueror. The truth is: You know what most guys were doing throughout Western history? Farming. That and maybe picking lice out of their hair and living to, oh, age thirty-five. But in the name of entertainment, people made up stories about men who did more than suffer and grow wheat.

So, here we are. Women on the verge of a new millennium. And whether our lives are actually interesting or not, we babes have every right to imagine ourselves as mavericks, adventurers, or conquerors.

If we start talking about stories we'd really like to see, eventually they'll seep into the national consciousness. Consider this: Just a few years ago, the phrase "You go, Girl" was exclusive to drag queens and homegirls. Now eighty-year-olds in Branson, Missouri, are calling it out to each other on bingo night.

In this day and age, talk alone has the power to influence our culture. The cutting edge can become a mainstream cliché in no time. And if you repeat a mainstream cliché long enough, it may even become an archetype.

Besides, Goddess bless our free-market economy, if we keep talking about the stories we'd really like to see, eventually some enterprising little bastard is going to pay attention.

Right now, the marketing departments of major corporations have scouts cruising the malls 24/7 trying to figure out what kind of sneakers girls consider cool, what kind of nail polish we're wearing, and what trend will result in the next big windfall. Plus, studies have shown that when a couple goes to movies, it's the woman who decides what they'll go see.

So greed is actually on our side. Companies *want* to market to us. Let's let it be known that cineplexes will sell more popcorn—and networks will sell more air time—by serving up something fresh and gender-bendy for us divas. Consider it a grass-roots cultural makeover, conducted by word of mouth.

To kick off this little campaign, let me offer up a few scenarios for movies that I, personally, would love to see.

1. *Latifah Weapon.* Queen Latifah stars as a special agent deployed to save Paris from a neo-Nazi terrorist cult. Janeane Garofalo is her white sidekick, who complains about having to crime-fight in high heels. "First thing I'm going to do when I catch those dickwads is stick their feet in a pair of Manolo Blahniks," she swears. "Comfortable shoes, my ass."

   In the middle of coolly rappelling down the side of the Eiffel Tower while being shot at by evil commandos, Latifah and Garofalo exchange flippant patter like:

   "Those suckers mess up my weave with their AK–47s and, let me tell you, I am blowing their asses to Jupiter." *Blam blam!*

   "That's a weave? Get out. I thought that was your real hair." *Blam blam!*

   "Oh my God, Girl. You don't know shit about black women's hair, do you?"

   Blam blam! "No. Guess I don't. I thought the only women with fake body parts were white blond chicks in Hollywood." *Blam blam!* "Well, there's two more facists who won't be cleaning their boots on our necks."

   After many gorgeous action sequences—in which our girls wipe out skinheads across the most scenic sections of Paris—Garofalo, being the white sidekick, gets shot, of course. But it's only a surface wound; Latifah comes to her rescue. ("Don't worry, little Girlfriend. I gotcha.") When the Medevacs arrive, Garofalo jokes that she did this on purpose to get out of wearing high heels. The movie ends when Garofalo gets released from the hospital; Latifah takes her to a salon to get a weave of her own. Everybody laughs. Fade until the blockbuster sequels, *Latifah Weapon II* and *Latifah Weapon III.*

2. *The Little Merman.* A Disney animated cartoon about a buff young "merman" from Sea World who falls in love with Sage, the fearless female captain of a Greenpeace ship. In order to win

Sage's love, the Little Merman makes a deal with an underworld sorcerer to trade his voice for a great pair of legs and buns. Sage does fall in love with him, seeing as he's the only guy she's ever met who actually *listens*. The couple sail off into the sunset together—with Sage at the helm, of course.

3. *Breezy Rider.* Two aging hippie chicks decide they've had it trying to be happy by using "healing crystals," rolfing, and St. John's Wort. So they take off across country on motorcycles instead. As they zigzag across America, they meet a renegade cheerleader alcoholic who joins them for a lot of groovy adventures, including crashing debutante cotillions, riding mechanical bulls in bars, picking up guys at Dollywood, and pissing off the Religious Right by streaking across the campus of Oral Roberts University. Features nifty motorcycle chase through the Mall of America, lots of smart dialog, and steamy love scenes between the heroines and way-buff Eagle Scouts half their age.

4. *Saving Ryan's Privates.* Five hundred thousand American women served as WACs and nurses in World War II. Surely someone can make a movie about their heroism and experiences with all the depth, power, and nuanced realism of Spielberg's epic. No weepies, please.

5. *Des Garçon du Lait* ("Milk Boys"). A touching French film about two poor, handsome young men who get a job delivering milk and cheese to a brilliant, eccentric widow living outside of town. As they take turns making deliveries, each of the milkmen falls in love with her. (Hey, the French are good at these May–August things.) One writes poems to her on the labels of the milk bottles. The other plays her music and paints her portrait on the brie wrappers. Being sensuous and wise, the widow teaches both of them, of course, about sex and life. The milk boys take turns being her love slaves and the three of them live happily after. (Think Matt Damon, Ben Affleck, and, say, Sophia Loren? Or Ryan Phillippe, James Van Der Beek, and

Anne Bancroft. This way her mature sexuality is exalted, not turned into a joke like it was in *The Graduate*.)

6. *Speed Rachel*. Speed Rachel is a gorgeous, gay, girl Mario Andretti. Behind the wheel of her race car, the Mach 7, Rachel races—and beats—legions of drivers whose minds are narrower than the tracks at the Indy 500. Her girlfriend, Trixie, cheers her from the sidelines. Since this movie has both lesbians and race cars, every guy on the planet should go nuts over it, too.

7. *Sisters from Another Planet*. A legion of high-tech, superso-phisticated female space fighters arrives in our galaxy and makes quick work of Earth's defense system. When their ships finally land in the US, it turns out, *tah-dah*: They're Puerto Ricans! And boy, are they pissed about the way the media has portrayed Hispanics down here in *Los Estados Unidos*—espe-cially Hollywood. So: payback time! (Rosie Perez stars in an all-Latino cast. None of this Meryl-Streep-in-a-black-wig shit.)

8. *Brooklyn Porn*. Basically, a conventional porno flick, except that (a) the penises are negligible, (b) fourteen hours' worth of cunnilingus instead, (c) everybody in them talks and moans with Brooklyn accents: *Owh gawd. Owh hawdah*. This way, gals who still feel guilty about their pleasures don't have to *pretend* to watch porn 'cuz it's funny.

9. *Hot Flashes*. Two menopausal women (Cecily Tyson and Bette Midler?) realize that, since our culture generally treats older women like they're invisible, they'd make excellent spies. And so they become brilliant counterintelligence agents—tracking down moles and spies across the globe. Each time the bad guys realize that the women are not Mary Kay saleswomen on hol-iday but master spooks packing heat, it's one more for the Girls' Team.

10. *Just Desserts*. Antonio Banderas in an ice-cream truck. Need we say more?

11. ***The Empress Strikes Back.*** I've always thought it was pretty arrogant for filmmakers to assume that in a galaxy far, far away, the world would still be dominated and saved by white guys. Sure, Princess Leia was a smartmouth leader in the original *Star Wars*, but there were those ridiculous danishes on her head, and by the end of *Return of the Jedi*, she had been relegated to eye candy. And Princess Naboo was given so little spunk, *she* might as well have been generated by a computer.

This movie takes place in a galaxy far, far away—but it's a galaxy ruled by Leia's great-granddaughters, a matriarchy of witty, agile princess fighters. They fly cool spacecraft, negotiate complicated intergalactic alliances with other species, work out their archetypal "mother issues" by fighting Diva Viper, hang out in bars full of fantastical muppets, come to the rescue of cute, helpless princes, and triumph in daring, spectacular battles with the forces of evil. Harrison Ford, meanwhile, spends the entire movie in shackles wearing nothing but a gold lamé Speedo bathing suit.

Now *that's* entertainment.

Chapter 20

ᎭᎭ

Play Like a Girl,
Watch Like a Girl

Like many young women, I grew up
believing that (1) physical ability
wasn't very important, and
(2) I didn't have any.

—JANICE KAPLAN

Oooh, I am just lovin' this whole women's team sports thing. How about US women's soccer? Can those women kick butt or what? And tell me the WNBA isn't the coolest thing since PMS nail polish. It's such a brilliant antidote to all the sexism out there. Plus, hot damn it's fun. Every time I see a soccer match or a basketball game or any other women's team in action, I get a rush. And I've never been a sports fan before—or an athlete, for that matter. Title IX was completely wasted on me: When I was little, my idea of a "sport" was to twirl around the living room in a tutu. And gym class? The sole exercise I ever got was in faking a stomach ache. Only sadists could've dreamed up boys-against-girls dodge ball.

Until recently, the one real appeal of going to a baseball game to me was the fact that you could shout "hot dog" in the middle of the stadium and have some guy run up forty flights of steps to serve it to you. And football? Ugh. Just another penis contest: Guys jump all over each other, then argue about who has more inches. I mean, how original is *that?* And okay, sure, I got into Michael Jordan—but so did about four billion other people who otherwise didn't watch much basketball.

Part of my disinterest, I realize, stemmed from the fact that sports' appeal is largely vicarious. Sports fans identify personally with the athletes; you put yourself in the players' sneakers, experiencing their trials and triumphs as your own.

But when you're a chick, sometimes it's hard to put yourself in someone else's sneakers if they're a size fourteen.

Now that women are playing professionally, it's a whole other ball game. Apathetic, pathetically femmey gals like me are now able to "get it"—to experience the thrill of sports, to admire the strategy, speed, and skill involved. For the first time in our lives, we're seeing ourselves on the playing field—as national heros.

I watch soccer matches on television now. I've happily sat through a documentary on Tennessee's legendary women's basketball coach, Pat Summitt. Best yet, I'm going to WNBA games with my other newly enthusiastic girlfriends. We shout "You go, Girls!" at the home team, boo the referees, and do the funky chicken in the stands, hoping to get on the Teletron.

Granted, we watch like girls. My friend Bari and I get weepy when the players come out. We get *farklempt* when the national anthem gets played. We get weepy *and farklempt* when the players actually begin to play. Dear Goddess, you'd think we were watching an opera.

But we're all just so damn proud to see these legions of cool, muscular, powerhouse women leaping and dashing and throwing and scoring. We're thrilled to see women being cheered for their strength and skill instead of for, say, their breast implants. And it touches us to the core to see this cheering coming from both sexes—but especially from girls.

Because by now we all know the benefits of girls *playing* sports. We know that it fosters confidence and coordination, teamwork skills and physical strength. Studies have shown that young women who play are more likely to do better in math and science, and less likely to become sexually active at a young age or stay with a guy who beats them.

But there's something to be gained for girls by *watching* women's sports, too, by supporting them with our hard-earned shekels and cheering them on from the stands.

Front guards make far better role models than fashion models do. In a culture where movie stars are currently trying to "out-diet" each other to fit into a size zero—a size *zero!*—it is beyond fabulous that young girls are now able to see women who are competing to outdo each other on the basis of their *strength*. When the members of the US Women's Soccer Team were introduced during the 1999 World Cup, my girls and I went batshit because each player's height and weight was announced—and they were life-sized! They were gals who weighed in at more than 120 pounds and showed muscles, not ribs!

It's also crucial for those of us with XX chromosomes to watch, because the fate and fortunes of women's professional sports really depend on us. If we come out for games and demonstrate that women's professional sports are highly lucrative, then the leagues will continue to grow. By asserting ourselves as a demographic, we can do the equivalent of getting a hot-dog vendor to climb forty rows to serve us—except on a national, prime-time, multimillion-dollar level.

Plus, any collective interest in women's sports pisses off the far right, who keep whining that antidiscrimination laws like Title IX are unfair or unnecessary, and that all women are really interested in are babies, feelings, and marriage.

But more important, for so long, we girls have cheered for boys. We've cheered as cheerleaders, groupies, voters, wives. Certainly, we've cheered out of a genuine desire to see our guys succeed. But we've also cheered from a position of weakness—because there were certain things we weren't allowed to succeed at ourselves. We've cheered for heroes we couldn't ever be, for teen idols we could never have, for contests we weren't eligible for, and for leadership that excluded us. Women have a very long history of cheering from the sidelines: For years, we understood that this was the closest we'd ever be allowed to get to center stage or center field. I mean, why else would we kill to be on the pom-pom squad? For our résumés?

But now, for the first time in history, we can cheer for our own. And the guys are cheering with us! And let me tell you: At the WNBA games, our own voices sound different. They're more alto than soprano. There's no hysteria or desperation in them. They resonate with pride, power, and ownership.

Granted, professional women's sports have been around for a while now. But until recently, they've been backup dates—or, in the case of figure-skating, treated like the athletic equivalent of chick flicks.

And until now, most of the female athletes who *have* captured the national spotlight have been, frankly, variations on ballerinas. They've been gymnasts: tiny, anorexic-looking girls balancing like exotic birds on a high thin beam. Or figure skaters, twirling prettily in sparkly costumes. Or graceful tennis players in little skirts.

Moreover, these athletes have been loners, not team players. As those sudsy TV bios show us, a lot of girls start training for the Olympics before they're even ready for training bras. By the time they've reached junior high school, they've moved away from their friends and families to live in a gym. They train 24/7 with Roumanian coaches and play Beat the Clock against their own puberty. And then, when they do win the gold, they win alone. It's just them out there on the ice, the court, the mat. Inadvertently, their stories reinforce a message that young women receive too often already: If you're going to be a strong, powerful woman, you're going to be alone.

No wonder the Spice Girls were such a hit with the girls! We gals crave our own dream teams! Sure, we want to be fabulous in our own right, but we'd like some camaraderie in our glory! We want leagues of our own!

Well, hallelujah. Finally, we're starting to get them—both as athletes and as, ahem, athletic supporters. There's a whole new sisterhood to be forged—and mercifully without the folksingers.

Of course, women's professional sports have not come close to occupying the place that men's sports do in our culture. But it's a start. And if we keep root-root-rooting for our Home Teams, our little sisters and daughters (not to mention our little brothers and sons) will grow up in a world where it's not only taken for granted that girls play ball fiercely, but that they can make a career out of it. Perhaps girls' teams can finally start pullin' in some of the big bucks that the boys get—more fab athletic scholarships, lucrative endorsements, and big-ass salaries! And more and more "soccer moms" will be women who kick it at the Olympics while their kids cheer them from the stands.

And not only will the high road be open to us, but the low one as well.

We too can experience the thrill of standing outside in five-degree weather with half our torso painted blue, the other half painted silver, and a sixteen ounce beer in each hand, as we shout "Detroit sucks!" at the top of our lungs. We, too, may have the thrill of mooning the Teletron before being hustled out of the stadium by a couple of humorless security guards. We, too, can enjoy the challenge of creating elaborate and inpenetrable spread sheets for office betting pools. We, too, can get so upset after our team loses that we punch a wall and break our hand—thereby inspiring a peculiar mixture of respect, pity, and fear among our colleagues when we come to work with a sling. We, too, can go nuts over all that groovy crappola sports fans can buy—the T-shirts, the hats, the foam fingers, the battery-powered light-up sweatshirts.

For "sexual equality" shouldn't just mean having to outperform men to prove that we're just as competent. It should also mean that we get to revel in all of our society's tribalism and silliness and stupidity and joy!

So I say, let's take ourselves out to that ball game and get out the greasepaint!

Or, just as good, let's invite the crew over and tell our loved ones that we can't do the dishes right now *because the game's on.*

And then we can sit back in our Lay-zee-Girl recliners with our clicker and our Diet Coke—and shout at the television, as people who resemble *us* play some serious ball—and feel pretty damn fantastic.

Chapter 21

൭

Give Us That Ol'-Time Religion—So We Can Clobber Sanctimonious Morons with It

The Bible contains 6 admonishments to homosexuals and 362 admonishments to heterosexuals. This doesn't mean God doesn't love heterosexuals. It's just that they need more supervision.

—LYNN LARNER

Y ou know, when it comes to Bible stories, I think our girl Eve has really gotten a bum rap. She is constantly painted as this evil temptress because she ate fruit from the Tree of Knowledge of Good and Evil, then convinced Adam to have a bite. But how hard must that have been, really, seeing as she was standing there *naked*? Heck, she could've told Adam to eat the snake and he would have gone: *Sure, okay. Whatever you say, Babe.*

Besides, it's thanks to Eve that, instead of living like blind, infantilized playthings in a garden, we humans are morally conscious and capable of thinking for ourselves.

I thought of Eve the other day as I was reading a speech written by humorist P. J. O'Rourke—an ex–*Rolling Stone* reporter who seems to do quite a lot of thinking for himself. In his speech, delivered at a Cato Institute conference, O'Rourke argued that collective wealth is bad, capitalism is good. He based his argument on—what else—the Bible.

In his speech, O'Rourke argued that the Ten Commandments actually instruct folks to become free-market capitalists. The way he sees it, he said, the final commandment (which basically says: Thou shall not covet they neighbor's stuff) implies that people shouldn't dream of making their neighbor's stuff their own: They should get up off their lazy asses, earn their own damn money, and buy their own damn stuff.

Wow. Simplistic little *moi*, I thought that the Tenth Commandment meant: *Keep your hands off your brother's toys, you idiot. Jealousy and stealing are bad!*

But his speech got me thinking. Not about people making their own fortunes, but about people thinking for themselves and using their own interpretations of the Bible to justify arguments before the Cato Institute—and everywhere else, for that matter. And it struck me that those of us with XX chromosomes have not been doing this nearly enough—even though you'd think it would be our birthright and all, seeing as we're supposedly descended from that troublemaker Eve.

Western religion is a power tool in our culture, and we SmartMouth Goddesses have much to gain by drawing upon it for our own arguments—by using it as creatively and selectively as everybody else seems to do.

Now, I know that for young women today, religion is an especially touchy issue.

First of all, we have enough people already trying to tell us what to think.

Second, some of us Western gals find religion mind-numbingly boring. The Bible? Great cure for insomnia. Just start reading those *begats* and you're out like a light.

Others of us see that ol'-time religion as downright dangerous and oppressive. In the eternal game of boys-against-girls, traditional patriarchal piety has not exactly been on our side: It's taught women to think of God as a big vindictive Daddy in the sky. It's taught us that our bodies are shameful; that we should shut up and submit to men; that our sexuality is sinful; and that contraception and premarital sex are the moral equivalent of homicide. It's also been used to justify slavery, clitoridectomies, war, and "ethnic cleansing"—none of them big winners with us, either.

But.

Simply dismissing religion as a tool of sexist oppression overlooks another fundamental reality: The majority of us gals really get something out of it. At the Grammy Awards, our girl Lauryn Hill wasn't thanking God for nothing. Religion is *serious* business for many of us, "our lifesaver and our light," as a friend of mine says. And for centuries, it's been the Eves, not the Adams, who've made up the majority of lay people in houses of worship. Faith has helped women find strength, solace, comfort, and community in an often-brutal world.

Tellingly, when the Center for Gender Equality conducted a poll in 1998, it found that seventy-five percent of women now ranked religion as "very important" in our lives, up from sixty-nine percent just three years prior. Another eighteen percent said religion was "somewhat important."

So we twenty-first-century foxes are wise to recognize that, when it comes to religion, one woman's snooze is another woman's shackles. And another woman's shackles is another's salvation. No need to start a holy war over it.

That being said, however, I think it's shrewd to recognize that traditional religion is also a source of political and rhetorical *power*. It's about *legitimizing influence*. And in this way, it's something we're smart to take seriously and seize for ourselves.

For there hasn't been a war waged, a kingdom built, or a republic declared without its leaders claiming that it's "God's will." And the world is full of demagogues who have gotten away with advancing stupid or dangerous ideas because they've wrapped themselves in the cloak of religion.

For example: the Fetus Fanatics blowing up abortion clinics and killing doctors in the name of Christianity. Or that lunatic Reverend Fred Phelps, carrying Burn Fags signs and quoting the Bible at the funerals of people who have died of AIDS. Or the so-called Christian Coalition, using the patina of religion to justify a flat tax. (Excuse me, but just where in the scripture does it say, "And then God created a flat tax"? Nowhere—unless maybe P. J. O'Rourke is your pastor.) Or even the 2000 presidential race, in which a number of candidates who slashed social programs for poor kids nonetheless bragged about having Jesus on their speed dial.

Then there's my ultimate, personal favorite, Randall Terry, who started Operation Rescue back in the 1980s. Guess what Randall Terry was before he started mobilizing legions of Fetus Fanatics to go block abortion clinics? A used-car salesman. Now, most people don't even trust a used-car salesman to sell them a *Buick*, let alone a religious doctrine. But once Randall Terry picked up the Bible and started calling women "baby killers"—voilà! He was suddenly taken seriously—instantly transformed from a Pinto-pusher in a parking lot into a *reverend* in a parking lot outside a clinic.

Talk about being "born again." Frankly, it's enough to make you lose your religion.

But there's a lesson to be learned in this, Girls: Wrap ourselves in piety and we'll never need another makeover.

Now, in the past three decades, many feminists who've had it with the sexism and abuses of Western religion have decided to take their toys and go play in their own spiritual sandbox. They've embraced Wicca, paganism, naturalism, and New Age spirituality. They've encouraged us to celebrate our cycles, worship our inner warrior, run with our wolves, and build our own temples.

Creating a spiritual life on our own terms certainly has its appeal. I mean, if I, personally, could invent my own religion, it might include, say, taking "communion" with M&M's and Yoo-hoo, and teaching men that cunnilingus is a form of prayer. (Heck, if they're going to be down on their knees anyway, they might as well do something useful.) In addition to the Ten Commandments, I'd have the Ten Strongly Worded Suggestions, including:

1. Thou shalt not whine.

2. Thou shalt not complain that you are oppressed if, in fact, you're part of the most privileged group of people in the history of the world.

3. Thou shalt maintain a body weight at least equal to your IQ.

4. Thou shalt not cheat at Scrabble.

And so forth.

The only problem with this do-it-yourself approach, however, is that it cedes all the power of traditional religion to the conservatives.

Right now, some truly scary right-wing nuts are acting like they've cornered the market on religious truth and morality. And to a large degree they have, if only because the rest of us have been hesitant to touch Western theology and wield it in our own arguments.

The whole Monica Lewinsky scandal a few years back was a good example of this. The right wing insisted President Clinton was the anti-Christ because he broke the commandment "Thou shalt not commit adultery." And it's true that Clinton was a cheating, lying horn-dog. No defending him there. But at the same time, the right wing was using dubious tactics to sling mud, circulate rumors, and prolong a biased investigation. Yet nobody ever said, "What about that other commandment, 'Thou shalt not bear false witness against thy neighbor'? That's on God's Top Ten list, too."

Maybe if someone had pointed out that religious rhetoric could cut both ways, politicians would think twice about exploiting it to score political points.

So I say: It's time to fight fire and brimstone with fire and brimstone.

The Bible is layered with meaning. (Ironically, guys like Jerry Falwell insist on interpreting the Good Book very literally. But put them in front of *Teletubbies*, and suddenly they become masters of subtext, cultural analysis, and innuendo. Go figure.) The Bible contains the most powerful and enduring stories of our culture. Plus, maybe I'm being naive, but it ultimately seems to promote justice, forgiveness, love, and redemption far more than finger pointing. So why should we progressive prima donnas ignore or relinquish it?

If a used-car salesman can exploit religion to promote his own misogyny—or if an ex–*Rolling Stone* reporter can use the Ten Commandments to promote yahoo free-market economics—certainly we gals can use them to promote human rights and our own politics. Female-centered religions may be good for the soul, but, let's face it: Beginning an argument with "According to Wiccan tradition . . ." ain't gonna score us any points on *Meet the Press*.

Next time some anti-choicers tell us, "The Bible says, 'Thou shalt not kill,'" maybe we should counter that the very same set of commandments also says, "Honor thy father and mother." Which means that a mother should be accorded special status and respect. She should not be viewed interchangeably with her fetus—or sacrificed for it, thank you.

If some professional homophobe starts quoting, say, 18 Leviticus, 1 Romans, or 6 Corinthians—the passages generally seen as prohibiting homosexuality—we might respond that *we'd* like to quote them all the sections in the Bible that talk about being merciful and loving—except that there are simply *too many* to memorize.

In fact, since Saint Paul tends to be a favorite of gay-baiting evangelicals, maybe we should ask them if they endorse slavery, like Saint Paul does in his Epistle to Philemon. We might ask free-market Bible thumpers if they have bank accounts or investments; Paul and Jesus came out pretty strongly against charging or accruing interest on money. For that matter, if we hear rabbis quoting the Torah to justify discrimination against gays and women, maybe we should ask 'em if they also believe in the Torah's stoning of adulteresses and in animal sacrifices.

But wait—it gets better! When hate-mongers claim that AIDS is a judgment from God, perhaps we should point out that Jesus spent a lot of time hanging out with lepers and prostitutes—the Biblical equivalent of an at-risk population. Were Jesus alive today, it's likely that many of his followers would be HIV-positive. In fact, Jesus himself sounds like just the kind of guy who'd decide to lead an AIDS walk—right over the Sea of Galilee!

Or, we might agree that maybe AIDS *could be* a judgment from God—but it's every bit as likely that AIDS is God's way of judging whether humans have learned to be more compassionate in the past two thousand years—whether, with all our piety, science, and resources, we've finally learned to "turn the other cheek" and practice true "Christian" compassion by caring for the sickest and most ostracized in our society.

(Of course, if this is the case, then it's the folks with the Kill Fags signs who may have a little explaining to do.)

Granted, our ideas will certainly enrage some people. But isn't that the point? I mean, part of the beauty of religion is that it has the power to inspire folks *or* get them hopping mad in no time. The point is to inspire or get them hopping mad in new ways, for new reasons, on our SmartMouth Goddess terms.

And if people accuse us of blasphemy—if they can't handle us being our own women and thinking for ourselves theologically— well, then, I say we just tell 'em that we're taking after our groovy foremother, Eve. And do we have an apple for them.

Chapter 22

ᕙᕗ

How to Handle Lunatics, Perverts, and Right-Wing Republicans

Give a man a free hand, and he'll try
to put it all over you.
—MAE WEST

A few months ago, I walked into a shoe store to try on a pair of fabulous, decadent high heels. They looked gorgeous, but my feet would've felt less pain if I'd dropped a television set on them.

"What's wrong?" said the salesman, as I hobbled and winced. "You don't like 'em? They look great on you."

"But they feel terrible," I gasped, pulling them off.

"What are you talking about?" he said. "They're comfortable shoes."

"Not on me," I said.

"Look, I'm telling you, they're comfortable!"

"How would you know?" I asked. "You've never worn them."

"That's it," he said. "Outta my store, you stupid bitch. I know a comfortable shoe when I see it."

Aah, nothing like being a chick. The respect we get is overwhelming. Every day is a brand-new ride on the Misogyny Train.

Construction workers think comments like, "Ooh, Mommy. Nice titties," might actually make us want to go out with them.

Mechanics, male doctors, and salesmen talk to us as if we have Down's syndrome.

Politicians—most of whom will never know what it's like to bleed through their maxi pad while sitting on a white futon—or to beg for an epidural—believe they know best about what we should be allowed to do with our reproductive organs.

And then, of course, there is the unending assortment of ass pinchers, skirt chasers, obscene phone callers, heavy breathers, wolf whistlers, tit grabbers, droolers, gropers, stalkers, flashers, homophobes, voyeurs, players, and aspiring date rapists.

How can hip chicks defend ourselves against this daily onslaught of insult, discrimination, and harassment?

Whining ain't an option. Nor is cowering. Though we've gotta choose our battles, taking a stand is far better than taking it lying down.

Of course, thanks to all the unsung heroines before us, if someone treats us badly just because we have boobs, we can now seek retribution through one of America's favorite pastimes: suing. But court cases are all-consuming. Plus, they're not always a realistic option. I mean, what are we going to do about the dumb-ass who hangs around the parking lot of the Food Lion, shouting, "Hey, Girls! Wanna check out my hard drive?" Subpoena him? I mean, *really*.

For that matter, can we really sue the *American Standard*, Rush Limbaugh, the Heritage Foundation, Focus on the Family, and the Christian Coalition for sexual harassment solely on the basis of the policies they endorse? (Well, now, actually, *there's* an idea.)

Besides, there's something bloodless about signing an affidavit. If a guy hogs the armrest on an airplane and "accidentally" lets his fingers brush over our thigh, it's just more satisfying to hit him in the ribs with an umbrella than with a court order. (Just like battered women feel safer clobbering their abuser with a baseball bat instead of a restraining order.)

So, frankly, when it comes to dealing with lunatics, perverts, and right-wing Republicans, I'd like to see us divas get a little more creative, irreverent, and radical. Guys dis women because they think they can get away with it. They don't really expect us to fight back. So why not give them a taste of their own rotten medicine? Why not turn the tables on Men Who Behave Badly by taking the things we *know* freak them out and using them to, well, freak them out? Why not harass our harassers, dis our dissers, and wield a little pootie power over the politicians?

Certainly, we've got the element of surprise working in our favor.

Sure, it's unorthodox. And, yes, it may be a bit risky. Certainly, if an attack on us is physical, it's a whole other ball game. But if a guy is simply a nuisance, *not* a psychopath—a pest but *not* a stalker—offensive but *not* threatening—then maybe we can use some of our humor, guts, and imagination to pioneer a whole new SmartMouth Goddess approach to social and political self-defense. We could give the morons a run for their mommies.

1. **Harassing our harassers.** There can be enormous power and satisfaction to be gained by making harassers start to wonder just who the hell *they're* dealing with.

    Several years ago, I met a great guy on an airplane. We hit it off right away and talked for the entire eight-hour flight. We shared a cab from the airport and exchanged phone numbers. Two days later, he called me for a date.

    At 5:30 in the morning.

    "Are you up yet, Susie?" he shouted into my answering machine. "Are you awake? Why aren't you talking to me, Susie?"

    Needless to say, this totally creeped me out. Of course, I refused to call him back. *Don't encourage him*, I told myself.

    But two days later, he called again—this time at 5:15. And at 5:40. And again at 6:07. "Susie, why aren't you listening to me? Susie, I need you to be there, goddamn it!" he shouted.

    After I unplugged my phone in a panic and arranged to get

an unlisted number, I lived in a state of anxiety for a week: After all, the guy knew where I lived.

But eventually my fear grew into fury. Why should *I* be the one losing sleep? I thought. Why should *I* be staying at a friend's house and peering over *my* shoulder whenever I picked up my mail?

And so I called him back and confronted him.

At 4:30 in the morning.

"Are you up yet?" I screamed. "How dare you call me at five A.M? Don't you have any goddamn manners? *No one is to treat me that way, do you understand?* What the hell is your problem?"

Oh, I went on the warpath. For twenty minutes I ranted and raved. I was the Medea of MCI; I made Joan Crawford look like Mommie Teresa. I was vicious; I was hysterical. I was a lunatic.

And lemme tell you, Girls, I was the bomb. Because I scared the living shit out of him.

"Please calm down," he begged. "Please don't freak out."

Poor guy. Whatever psychodrama he'd been dreaming up, it certainly hadn't occurred to him that *I* might want to audition for the psycho role.

Of course, I never heard from him again—despite the fact that Bell Atlantic sure took its sweet time changing my number.

For all their bravado, almost nothing terrifies guys more than being yelled at by a hysterical woman. They'll do almost anything to avoid having us go ballistic. As soon as they even see us *starting* to steam, they back off like maniacs: "Okay, just calm down. Calm down, Lady. Don't get all bent out of shape here."

In their minds, really, we're all just a few steps away from turning into that bunny-cooker in *Fatal Attraction*.

So there's something to be said for exploiting this, for fighting crazies with craziness, lunatics with lunacy.

Sure, we gotta be real careful. Some situations are riskier

than this one. And if there's already legal action involved, we probably don't want to go on the record screaming like a banshee on some moron's voice mail or getting in his face in front of an eyewitness.

But we got options, *Goils*, and they're not just victim or plaintiff. We can be as whack as the best of them. As Hunter S. Thompson said, "When the going gets weird, the weird turn pro."

2. **Don't say "no." Say "commitment."** Goddess only knows why, but after seven thousand years of "known" civilization, guys still seem to have trouble understanding the word "no." The word doesn't seem to have been downloaded into their thesauruses correctly. Say the word "no" to a guy, and half the time he thinks we're saying "maybe." Or, "try harder." Or, "not at this very moment, but check again in five minutes."

Luckily, there is one word that's like Guy Kryptonite. One word that makes even the pushiest, most persistent player cool down faster than a can of microwaved Beef-a-Roni.

That word is "commitment."

If some bozo keeps hitting on us—even after we've told him we're not interested—maybe we should say, "Okay. You wanna hook up with me? How about going shopping for china patterns next weekend and meeting my parents?" We should tell him that nothing turns us on more than a monogamous relationship in which we talk about our feelings with a guy— and he talks to us about his. We should mention the words "expectation" and "emotional needs" a lot. Or tell him how we like to page our man six or seven times each day just to ask, "Honey, what are you thinking?"

For extra protection, maybe we should carry a copy of *Modern Bride* magazine with us at all times. Consider it the anti-condom. If things with a date start getting out of hand, we can grab the magazine and wave it in front of him shouting, "Marriage! Commitment! Intimacy!"

The guy should be up and running so quickly, the door won't have time to hit him on the ass.

3. **Sarcasm is a girl's best friend.** Need to cool off a co-worker who's hot under the collar? An ounce of withering sarcasm could save us a bundle in legal bills and headaches: "Oh, my God, Jake, I had no idea you were trying out for the sexual-harassment Olympics! How ambitious of you! Tell me: Are you trying for a real live lawsuit, or do you just want to create a really uncomfortable work situation that will make both of us miserable and might get you fired?"

4. **Every "Cupcake" deserves a "Snookums."** If someone calls us "Honey," "Babe," or "Sweetheart," why not respond in kind? Say, "Yes, Poopsie," "Sure thing, my little *Chou Fleur*" (French for "cauliflower," if they care), "Anything you say, my little fuzzy-wuzzy wumpkin."

   If they get annoyed, we can explain that since they called us "Honey," we just assumed that using unprofessional, cutesy, belittling nicknames was their policy—and, hey, we are nothing if not team players, okay?

5. **Calling the catcallers on it.** When you're a girl growing up in this day and age, you learn pretty quickly that the only people besides your relatives who feel compelled to make unsolicited comments about your body are construction workers. And guys hanging out on the stoop. And truck drivers stuck at red lights. And men on subway platforms. And guys in pinstripe suits eating lunch around the fountains in midtown. And cops dunking donuts. And homeless men. And teenage boys waiting on line at the movie theater. And, oh, yeah, just about everybody else with a penis.

   You learn pretty quickly that to be a female between twelve and fifty means the male world generally regards you as a deaf beauty contestant—in a pageant in which every single one of them, of course, is wholly qualified to be a judge.

   Sometimes you can't go anywhere without setting off a chorus of whistles, catcalls, pornographic propositions, nasty comments, kissing noises, barking, derogatory remarks, ethnic slurs, sexual innuendos, and ratings games.

Is it any wonder that more women than men suffer from migraines?

The prevailing wisdom, of course, is to ignore the ignoramuses. But sometimes the constant harassment just wears a girl down. We end up walking around enraged, defensive, uncomfortable, and annoyed. And why should we suffer? We're not the ones with the verbal diarrhea here.

So while talking back might not curb the dogs, so to speak, it may at least help *us* to blow off some steam.

Suggested retorts:

"Get a life, get a job" used to work wonders for the homegirls in my neighborhood.

Ditto for, "Dream on, baby."

"Tell it to your mother" gives guys pause.

So does, "Yeah? Say that to your wife and daughters. See how much *they* appreciate a comment like that."

And something my co-worker used to say a lot: "You couldn't afford me."

Of course, with all of these we risk provoking the guys and escalating the exchange. So, obviously, we've got to choose our battles.

But my friends and I discovered a comeback that has served us well and seems to be all-purpose: "Suffer, baby."

It keeps us in a position of power, not defensiveness, and actually makes the guy laugh.

More important, it usually leaves him speechless, while we keep right on walking like *all that*.

6. **Don't fuck Republicans or anti-choicers.** Take it from those comedic Greeks. In Aristophanes' play *Lysistrata*, the women withheld their sexual favors from the men in order to put an end to the war between Athens and Sparta. By the end of the play, the guys were all hobbling around the Acropolis with huge erections, frantically brokering peace.

Well, now. For years, certain American men have been waging a war against women's sexuality and reproductive freedom. (Big surprise: Seventy percent of "pro-life" activist leaders are men, as are the majority of hard-core Republicans). So why should we put out for them?

Really. The fuck should stop here. Any guy who votes or works against our sexual freedom and equality—actively *or* passively—shouldn't be allowed to reap the benefits of it. Let him see that his politics have real consequences. If it's so important to him to control sexual activity and reproductive rights, let him start with his own. We'll be all too happy to help him.

I mean, we don't see too many Sistahs voluntarily sleeping with the Boyz in White Hoods, do we? Or Jewish chicks willingly bedding down with neo-Nazis? Why share our booty with someone who's trying to make it property of the US Government?

If a guy wants to enjoy our cookies, then let him defend our bakery, thank you.

7. **And if all else fails:** Knee 'em in the nuts. Hey, if guys are really going to abuse their sexual power, we gotta take it away from them. Goddess knows men don't think twice about preying on our physical vulnerabilities. Besides, if a guy's family jewels are so sacred, Mother Nature wouldn't have put 'em right out there in front, just dangling in the wind, in the direct line of our fabulous kneecaps.

Chapter 23

๑๑

Onward, Vixen Soldiers!

In politics, if you want anything said,
ask a man. If you want anything done,
ask a woman.
—MARGARET THATCHER

Okay, here's a joke.

In a medieval town, two men and a woman are about to be beheaded.

When the first man is brought to the guillotine, the executioner points to the neck rest and asks, "Do you want to look up at the blade or down away from it?"

"Down away from it," says the man.

The executioner places the man's head facedown in the neck rest and pulls the cord. Lo and behold, the blade doesn't fall! The executioner and the attending priest concur that this is a miracle.

"God has clearly intervened to spare your life!" they tell the prisoner. "Go! Live in peace with the king's forgiveness!"

The second man is brought to the execution block.

"Do you want to look up at the blade or down away from it?" the executioner asks.

"Down away from it," says the second man.

The executioner places the man's head facedown in the neck rest and pulls the cord. Again, the blade doesn't fall! Again, the executioner and the priest exclaim, "This is a miracle! God has clearly meant to spare your life! Go! Live in peace with the king's forgiveness!"

Then the woman is brought to the block.

"Do you want to look up at the blade or down away from it?" the executioner asks.

"Up at it," she says.

The executioner places her faceup in the guillotine and pulls the cord. And again! The blade doesn't fall!

"Another miracle!" the executioner and the priest shout.

"Oh, no, I see the problem," says the woman, pointing up. "The blade's just stuck. Pull a little harder."

This joke, told to me by another woman, made me groan: *A woman staring right up at the blade, helping it along*? Oh, Girls. Let's face it: Sometimes, that's exactly what we do.

Don't get me wrong. Unlike conservatives, I don't get my jollies blaming the poor, oppressed, and downtrodden for being poor, oppressed, and downtrodden. Nor do I believe that we gals get what we deserve in the gender-equity sweepstakes.

But too often, when women are already on the executioner's block, I see us lying there, staring straight up at the blade, and in our eagerness to prove that we're intelligent and cooperative, that we're nice and accommodating and good sports, we help that blade right along.

I can't tell you how often I've heard white friends say, "Well, I'm not a *feminist* or anything, but . . ." Or sisters say, "Hey, *feminism* is for white girls." Or straight girls say, "Feminists are man-hating lesbians." Or young career women say, "Feminism is so over."

The modern women's-rights movement may have been going on for decades, yet we're still reluctant to go to bat for ourselves politically or assert ourselves as a social force. Our attitude seems to be culled not from the pages of *Ms.* magazine but from *Mad*: "What, Me Worry?" We're a generation of Alfred E. Neumans—albeit with old "Girl Power" T-shirts and nose rings.

Why are so many young, straight *women* willing to feminist-bash these days?

I guess we can dismiss Katie Roiphe as a lobotomized narcissist. (Her work does seem to follow the formula of, "If it happened to me and two Harvard friends, it's reality!") And Elizabeth Wurtzel not only admits that she *is* on drugs but actually writes books about them. As for Wendy Shalit, the modesty maniac, well, c'mon. It's easy to tell other women to keep their legs crossed when *you've* never been so giddy with lust that you've walked into a lamp post.

But for others, feminism's traditional concerns are decidedly *WW*—wealthy and white. *(You want the right to work outside the home? Hey, most of us have been doing that for centuries, thank you . . . You say religion is sexist? Well, where do you think I get my strength?)*

For still others, it rankles us stylistically. We find it *WWW*—Wealthy, white, and *whiny*. I mean, how many Take Back the Night rallies can a girl really stomach? Speaking out against violence against women is critical, but hear about victimhood long enough, and eventually you just want to go buy a lipstick and call it a day.

Friends of mine with kids, of course, feel feminism ignores motherhood and denigrates their choices. Still others believe that being a feminist, like being a liberal, has been maligned by our government, the media, and men because it threatens our nation's traditional values and right-wing agenda.

Also, feminism is an easy target, a ready-made scapegoat for anyone who's unhappy with the way things are going in this world. *Real* agents of negative changes in family life over the past thirty years have been vast abstract entities, such as corporations, the shifting economy, globalization, and urban sprawl. As muckraker

Michael Moore points out, more Americans believe the world is run by corporations then by the president, but most of us can't name the CEO of Exxon. So, it's far easier to blame Gloria Steinem for women's frustrations because, hey, at least she has a face.

Yet some of our ambivalence toward feminism, I believe, also stems from the fact that straight women, unlike any other oppressed group in the world, are in the unique position of being emotionally involved with our "oppressors."

Yeah, we want equal rights and personal power. But we also want love and partnership. *And we've been taught that the two sets of needs are mutually exclusive.* A powerful woman, we're taught, is not desirable. She's a ballbuster. She's ugly. She's humorless. She's unsexy. She's Alexandra on *Josie and the Pussycats*—the aggressive, dateless villain with a streak of gray in her hair. Or Daria, who's sharper than Lorena Bobbit's cutlery but equally unpopular with the guys. Or, to deal in *real* life for a moment: Martha Stewart. Ms. Stewart is certainly no more annoying and self-aggrandizing than Donald Trump, but the media has harped on *her* abrasive personality, single-hood, and failed marriage even more than it's harped on his.

We girls get the message and we get it early: Strong women don't get the guys. Stand up for yourself and you stand alone.

And no other oppressed group has the privilege of this delightful Catch-22, of thinking that they have to choose love *or* power, helplessness *or* loneliness, basic emotional needs *or* fundamental freedoms. African-Americans don't worry that if they speak out against racism: *Oh! Gee! White people won't like us!* Homosexuals don't worry that no one will date them because of their politics. Hispanics don't fear that by embracing Latino culture, they'll never get laid.

But straight women? We worry that if we say we're a feminist, *no one will want us.*

Can you blame us, then, for our reluctance?

But.

Let's flip through our reality checkbook for a moment, shall we? Just who are all the famous, lonely, bitter feminists that the world is so quick to vilify?

Gloria Steinem, who's had numerous wild affairs and marriage proposals? Susan Sarandon? Elizabeth Dole? Oprah Winfrey? Naomi Wolf? Patricia Ireland? Mavis Leno? Alice Walker? Susie Bright? Catherine MacKinnon? Wendy Kaminer? Pat Schroeder? Anna Quindlen? Queen Latifah? Cybill Shepherd? Roseanne? Drew Barrymore?

These women are living proof that bodacious feminist broads who speak their minds get their goodie bags, too.

So we Third Wave babes would be wise to dispense with our fears and recognize that we've inherited some incredibly hard-won freedoms from gals who came before us. And these privileges don't exempt us from their upkeep.

After all, sexual discrimination, unfortunately, has not gone the way of the eight-track tape. Women today are shouldering a dis-proportionate share of the burden of raising families *and* bringing home the bacon. We still earn less money than the guys. Child care sucks. Fetus Fanatics are blowing up women's health clinics and killing doctors in the name of "defending life." Men are totally confused and bent out of shape about masculinity. All the "isms" are alive and kicking. Health care is discriminatory. And if we took a group photo of the people in the highest positions of power in American corporations and the United States Government, it would still look like a gentlemen's country club in Greenwich, Connecticut.

Besides, while we might see ourselves as "not just women but human beings," there are a lot of politicians and religious leaders out there who don't. In their eyes, we gals are "naturally" destined to be wombs and homemakers—and if we don't agree, well, they'll try to pass legislation to make it so. (Unless, of course, we're poor. Then they'll pass laws to keep us from "sitting at home doing noth-ing.") So our rights are like muscles—if we don't flex 'em, exercise 'em, and keep 'em strong, they'll be history. Use 'em or lose 'em.

Yeah, the politics of victimhood are wearying. Given a choice, many of us would rather spend our precious time enjoying our freedom instead of defending it. But we can't afford the luxury of complacency. As actress Carrie Fisher once said, "You never reach the point where you say, 'Okay, I'm successful now. I might as well take a nap.'"

Besides, somebody's gotta rule the world, so why the hell shouldn't it be us?

We may just need to give political activism a makeover of sorts. Because, frankly, holding hands and singing "Kumbaya" ain't doin' it for us. Ditto for standing in the rain with a Stop Rape placard. I mean, why do that when we can e-mail our congressperson and volunteer at the women's shelter? Our generation's tools and sensibilities are different. And so we should adopt and adapt political activity so that it's viable and relevant to *who* we are in our lives and times. No reason to become a generation lost in cyberspace, after all.

And so, to this end, allow me to suggest a few humble "makeover" tips:

1. **Choose our battles.** Nobody can fight racism, deliver meals to people with AIDS, and protect the rain forest all at once. That's a good recipe for burnout. So is viewing the world in absolute terms. Let's just pick one or two causes apiece that we want to champion and stick with 'em. A recent study comparing conservative and liberal foundations revealed that the conservative ones are more effective because they concentrate their efforts. Good leftie organizations tend to spread themselves too thin. So let's focus our efforts so they can be sustained over the long haul.

2. **Think small.** My roommate and I once put "Get Life, Save World, Win Nobel Peace Prize" on our to-do list. It was noble but deluded. Being a Big Sister to a little girl—or teaching self-defense to elderly women—is simply more feasible than "overthrowing the patriarchy."

3. **Show 'em the money.** Since "money talks"—and since we chicks are accused of never shutting up in the first place—why not become financial yentas? If we have some extra moolah,

let's put it where our mouth is to promote our best interests. Maybe this means helping poor mothers purchase business suits for job interviews. Or supporting a cool woman who's running for Congress. Or taking a page from our Korean sisters and pooling our wealth to help each other launch businesses.

If we can donate just ten dollars a month to promote a cause we believe in, that's one hundred and twenty dollars a year. If we can team up with, say, nine of our friends, that's twelve hundred dollars annually. So for the price of a couple of magazines apiece, even those of us in entry-level jobs can wield some real clout. Why leave all the power to capitalist tools like Steve Forbes? Hell, his idea of "justice" is a flat tax.

4. **Don't believe the hype.** Our culture gives us every opportunity to dumb ourselves down or numb ourselves out. It's easy to succumb to the lulling fantasies of TV's Almighty Cathode Ray Nipple. It's also easy to get disgusted by the whole enterprise and tune out. But being a powerful woman in America demands that we remain conscious and self-educated. So we gotta read the newspapers, the alternative publications, and surf the Net for substance. Let's know our enemies, too: Check out stuff like the *American Spectator* or the *National Review.* (Just don't try to read them while you're eating.)

5. **Exit the comfort zone.** The ability to work with people whom we don't like is crucial to our success—though, ironically, human impulse always seems to go against this. Whenever I myself am confronted with, say, a twenty-two-year-old Young Republican smoking a cigar, my instinct is to high-tail it into the next room for the sake of preserving world peace.

How-evah. While surrounding ourselves with people who think and feel like we do is good for the old self-esteem (and blood pressure), we cannot live our entire lives trying to replicate and revive Lilith Fair. Learning to deal with adversity and difference will serve us far better in the long run than trying to exist exclusively with like-minded people. So whether this means reaching out to immigrant communities, co-sponsoring an event with the chamber of commerce, or having lunch with the White Boy Republican, stepping out of the womb is vital. In fact, the more we step out of our comfort zone, the bigger it becomes.

6. **Get our pootie on the move.** Ironically, so many recipes for women's "empowerment" these days are couched in terms of, well, the couch. Books like *Chocolate for the Woman's Soul* send us on a journey inward, down the path of self-analysis.

They claim that what we gals tell ourselves, imagine for ourselves, and realize about ourselves will enable us to rule our own Magic Kingdom. We'll be co-dependent no more and make unfoolish choices. Best of all, we can obtain such power without ever getting off the sofa. Wow. Talk about a course in miracles. Talk about habits of highly effective people.

But c'mon! We SmartMouth Goddesses are wise to raise a well-shaped eyebrow at this stuff. Because women can't rule the planet if we haven't left our living rooms. To get powerful, it's better to put down the "creative visualization" books and get out of the house.

Right now, some twenty-three countries still prohibit women from getting a passport or traveling unless they have permission from a male relative. Never mind that, hello, it's the twenty-first century: Women in Qatar still have to ask Dad if they can borrow the car. Saudi Arabian women are not allowed to drive, period. And, thanks to the Taliban, our sisters in Afghanistan can't even leave the damn house by themselves without risking a beating.

Travel has always been a way of grooming men for power. In numerous cultures, preparing young men for leadership involves exposing them to an unfamiliar environment, whether this means sending them on a "walkabout" or to a sadistic English boarding school. It's no coincidence that many prestigious scholarships like the Rhodes and Fulbright require recipients to study in a foreign country. Mastery of the world requires, well, mastery of the world. Gotta feel comfortable in it.

And so, travel is a privilege and an educational opportunity that we Vixen Soldiers need to recognize, seize, and exploit wherever and whenever we can—be it through the Peace Corp, a road trip, or a fellowship—especially because so many women are hidden away, discouraged from venturing out, and relegated to the margins of public life. Learning about the world at large, and asserting ourselves as a visible presence in it, ultimately means more power to all of us—including those girls who stay home.

7. **Give leftie attitudes a makeover.** As far as activism goes, there's being Politically Correct (PC), and then there's Not Being an Asshole (NBA). Frankly, I'm voting for door number two these days.

Extreme PC-ism has a way of running people's passion, enthusiasm, and political fervor through a strainer until there's nothing left but gruel. And, frankly, it's killed some gals' appetites for activism altogether.

Political Correctness may have started out as an effort to make people more conscientious and sensitive about power, privilege, difference, and language, but there's a fine line between being sensitive and being thin-skinned, and I'm afraid that PC has reached the point of epidermal translucency. Yeah, if my gal from Japan prefers "Asian" to "Oriental," she's got my backing. Ditto for a person in a wheelchair who prefers "physically disabled" to "crippled." And I'm not for deliberately kicking dogs, exploiting Third World labor, or dumping toxic waste into the ocean, either.

But when animal-rights activists ask the village of Fishkill, New York, to change its name to Fishsave so as not to promote cruelty to trout, I mean, c'mon, people. This is a symptom of Too Much Free Time.

When a woman sues the Murfreesboro, Tennessee, city hall for sexual harassment because a painting of a half-nude woman in its rotunda "offended" her, she makes a mockery of laws designed to protect us gals from profoundly serious discrimination.

And when political discussions deteriorate into hairsplitting about who in the room is being oppressive and who's being oppressed, augh! Really, it's enough to make a girl a Libertarian.

If we're going to strive for a better and more diverse world, we've got to give the people in it a little room to breathe, misspeak, and be themselves.

8. **Make Susan B. Anthony proud.** A few years ago, I worked in a congressional office. We'd receive letters essentially like this:

Dear Congresswoman:

There's a toxic-waste dump in my backyard. Also, the schools are a mess, the roads are full of potholes, my family has no health care, and the noise from the airport is driving us crazy. Can't you do something about this? Also, I want lower taxes and smaller government. Congress sucks. It'll be a cold day in hell before you bastards get my vote.

Unfortunately, this reflects a logic that too many of us employ: The state of the world sucks, so I'm not voting for anyone who runs it.

Yeah, well, my grandmother had a motto: *If you don't vote, you can't complain.*

If we're unhappy with the status quo, we've got to use whatever tools are at our disposal, limited as they may seem. Frankly, we women have more to win—and lose—at the voting booth. We're more likely than men to depend on the government for health care and Social Security. We comprise two-thirds of all minimum-wage workers. Our reproductive and health-care decisions are largely up for grabs. And since we're the primary heads of households in a majority of American homes these days, we stand to benefit more from things like parental leave and public education—things brought to us by Yours Truly, the government. As long as politicians want to make our lives and bodies their business, we've got to make their business ours.

Besides, if you ask me, the right to complain is simply too precious not to defend.

9. **Let's make like the National Rifle Association.** Not with the guns, but with the single-mindedness. Because, ironically, we have a lot to learn from the NRA. The NRA may be mercenary and gun crazy, but they're a model of brilliant political organization. The NRA supports some outrageous and highly unpopular ideas, yet for decades they have gotten plenty of politicians to take them seriously and endorse truly psychotic legislation. (I mean, the Second Amendment calls for a "well-regulated militia," not for allowing every delusional, wife-beating yahoo to freely purchase an Uzi, thank you.)

   How has the NRA been so successful? It has a very clear idea of what's important to its members, then targets these issues for unwavering attention, money, and clout. It doesn't matter if a political candidate has brilliant stands on health care and education. If he or she supports, say, equipping guns with childproof locks, the NRA will oppose him or her. It will throw all its money (and it does have shitloads) and endorsements behind the opposing candidate, providing that *that* candidate thinks it's okay to allow a mentally unstable teenager to buy a Glock at a K-Mart. Then the NRA will summon its members to flood the polls on election day. And the members will come—and vote.

   Members from the NRA don't get caught up trying to prove to the rest of the world that they're not *just* gun nuts. They focus fervently on what's in their best interest, then lobby for it like maniacs. By doing so, they've remained one of the most powerful interest groups in America.

   We SmartMouth Goddesses would be smart to follow suit. Promote, vote, and lobby for our own best interests—unwaveringly, and without apologies.

10. **Why should the drag queens have all the fun?** There's no better form of subversion than *irreverence with breasts.* Humor is—and must always be—our ultimate power tool, our primo

weapon of choice. There's no quicker death knell for us progressive prima donnas than taking ourselves or the world too seriously. Quite frankly, if we don't see the brilliant silliness of it, or the comedy in our own existence, we're really not fit to defend or rule anything. Activist Emma Goldman once said, "If you can't dance to it, it's not my revolution." Well, the same is true for any "revolution" where we can't vamp it up, camp it up, parody, satirize, mock, rag, lampoon, goof, howl, hoot, cackle, chuckle, chortle, giggle, guffaw, shriek, play a kazoo, slap our knees, get hysterical, or laugh our asses off, either.

Besides, when author Margaret Atwood polled men about what they fear most from women, the men replied, "That they'll laugh at us." If that doesn't make it crystal clear what our strategy should be toward the patriarchs, frankly, I don't know what does.

Conclusion

So Who Ever Said We Were
Supposed to Be Happy?

It's always something.
—GILDA RADNER

In 1998, a woman named Danielle Crittenden wrote a book, *What Our Mothers Didn't Tell Us: Why Happiness Eludes the Modern Woman.* Its premise? That women today are "more miserable and insecure, more thwarted and obsessed with men, than the most depressed, lithium-popping suburban housewives of the 1950s."

Crittenden, who herself was never a fifties housewife, bases her claim on the fact that women's magazines—which, as we know, have absolutely no commercial agenda whatsoever—depict women as more desperate and confused now than twenty years ago.

Why does Crittenden believe women today are more "desperate and confused"? Because in our heart of hearts, she says, most young women really want to be wives and mothers more than anything—but "feminists" have convinced us to deny this.

If we get married and have children in our early twenties, stay home to raise them, then launch careers when we're middle-aged, Crittenden asserts, we'll be far happier than the Baby Boomers. These women, she argues, are bitter and miserable because feminists told them to have careers first, then families, in a way that goes against female "nature" and "biology."

An eye roll, please.

Okay, let's ignore a few things for a moment.

Let's ignore that a 1999 poll of such Baby Boomers by *Redbook* magazine found that women today "report an enormous contentment" and say their lives are "getting better all the time."

Let's ignore that divorce rates are higher for those who marry young.

Let's ignore that most mothers today, no matter what their age, *have* to work (the average income for an American family is a whopping thirty-nine thousand dollars).

Let's even ignore that we gals have brains as well as wombs—and, last time I checked, brains were a part of female "nature" and "biology," too.

And since we SmartMouth Goddesses are a generous sort, let's even assume that, for those of us who know for certain by age twenty-two that we want kids more than anything, there are plenty of mature twenty-two-year-old men ready, willing, and able to single-handedly support us for the next fifteen years.

Even if we perform all these stunning contortions of logic, Crittenden's argument still falls flat. Why?

Because it assumed there's a special reason why "happiness eludes the modern woman" in the first place.

Excuse me, but people have been miserable and neurotic since time immemorial. Who told Crittenden that we modern gals are supposed to be exempt?

Throughout history, our species has been a bunch of kvetching, existentially insecure, anxious, semipsychotic pains in the ass. We've suffered from something known as "the human condition," which is sort of like a global, eternal form of PMS.

And why shouldn't we? We're the only species that can comprehend its own mortality and yet do absolutely nothing to change it. I mean, talk about a cosmic joke where we're the punch line.

The human condition means that, like any other animal, we worry about survival issues, such as getting enough food, until the moment when we get enough food—at which point, unlike any other animal, we immediately start worrying about stuff like "good cholesterol" and whether Corn Bugles are better than Fritos.

The human condition means that once we stop worrying about getting raped and pillaged by marauders, we start worrying about stuff like 401(k) plans and male-pattern baldness.

The human condition means that, if we're not trapped suburban housewives addicted to lithium in the 1950s, we're neurotic career girls popping Prozac in the 2000s.

In other words, as Gilda Radner's brilliant *Saturday Night Live* philosopher Rosanne Rosannadanna used to say: "It's always something."

We gals are smart to acknowledge this. The fact that we're human predisposes us to a certain amount of angst. *This* is a given. As my mother always told me: "You make your choice, you pay your price. Everyone."

My dentist recently engaged me in a big discussion of feminism. Actually, who are we kidding here? She talked, I drooled. I was a captive audience in that damn chair.

"Women are juggling so much, now," my dentist said. "They're up at 5:30 A.M to get the kids to day care, earn money, do the housework. They're working so hard."

I wanted to rip the paper bib off my chest, spit the little suction tube out of my mouth, and cry, "Women have always worked hard and juggled! It used to be, we were up at five-thirty in the morning to milk the fucking cows, gather eggs, and help till the land—otherwise, *we didn't eat*. We worked all day farming, mothering, and running the household. We routinely buried at least half our children and died in childbirth ourselves. And, to top it all off, we had to endure all sorts of humiliation and abuse because we were entirely dependent upon men for survival, social acceptance, protection, and money!"

Goddess only knows where Americans got the cockamamie idea that, in the "good old days," women stayed home and "didn't work." The much-mythologized, stay-at-home middle-class American housewife of the 1950s existed for maybe twenty-five of the seven thousand years of recorded Western history. I mean, that's hardly a trend, people.

Besides, since when is homemaking not work? Just because an oven is self-cleaning doesn't mean the rest of the house can take care of itself. The whole reason those glorified fifties housewives began celebrating happy hour at 11:00 A.M. was largely because no one was recognizing or legitimizing their contributions to society.

But I didn't say all of this to my dentist. It's amazing how quickly one abandons one's principles when there's a drill in one's mouth.

Look, feminism has given us choices. It's given us more ways to be happy and, yes, more ways to be miserable. But now, at least, we get to choose our destiny a little more. I mean, c'mon! Are we naive enough to think that there's some magic formula, some code-cracking combination of life decisions that will guarantee us nirvana—if only we're smart enough to make the right choices?

In case we *are* that naive, here's a handy-dandy laundry list of some of our options, complete with upsides and downsides. Out of respect for Danielle Crittenden, I've started with her formula first. Here goes:

Formulas for Happiness

1. Marry & have kids young, stay home, launch career late.

Pros: Makes most of biological clock & stamina. More able to chase toddler through traffic while carrying stroller, diaper bag, breast pump.

Cons: If hubby departs, you might as well be on *Titanic.* Either way, have fun competing against 21-year-olds for entry-level jobs during menopause.

2. Career first, marriage & kids later.

Pros: Earn own money, acquire stolen office supplies & frequent-flier miles from work. Possibility of Having It All at Once.

Cons: Including nervous breakdown. Kids maybe conceived in petri dish. Stepping on squeaky toys in high heels at age forty-four makes you slowly homicidal.

3. Be trophy wife to really rich guy.

Pros: Don't ever have to worry about money again. Permanent reservations at Le Cirque 2000.

Cons: Requires constant plastic surgery; essentially glorified prostitute.

4. Single-career powerhouse.

Pros: Money, professional fulfillment. When people ask, "Why no kids?" can respond, "Because I'll be hiring yours."

Cons: Stock portfolios can't clean kitchen, perform oral sex.

5. Single mom.

Pros: Get to have family even w/o romantic partner. Piss off Dan Quayle.

Cons: Harder than it looks on TV. Harder than anything else in world. Fast track to poverty.

6. Be countercultural.

Pros: Live on own terms, buck oppressive system, groovy & interesting clothes & friends.

Cons: How much tofu can person eat? Also, good luck getting health insurance.

7. DINKS: Dual Income No Kids.

Pros: Can dine at restaurants w/o chicken fingers on menu, travel to Zimbabwe, never have to listen to Barney video.

Cons: Perpetually on defensive. Treated like freaks. Greek chorus asking, "So when are you going to have children?"

Really. I say we Supergirls should just be glad we have the fundamental American freedom to fuck up our lives entirely on our own terms.

Besides, new studies suggest that genetics are as responsible for a person's level of happiness as anything else. If this is in fact true, then today's miserable Baby Boomer career women would probably have been just as miserable pushing a baby carriage back in the 1950s. And the June Cleaver prototypes who had orgasms over their self-cleaning ovens in 1957 would probably be just as ecstatic over cell phones and corporate careers in the year 2001.

We gals are living during a Golden Age for women right now. Sure, just like any other time in history, ours has its wars, disease, brutality, crappy food, boring jobs, screaming children, loneliness, heartbreak, cockroaches, disappointments, fear, annoyances, oppression, and jerks.

Sure, we're required to be courageous and responsible in new ways. But so what? Like we really have anything better to do than grow up and take charge?

We shouldn't let anybody—be it a bunch of neoconservative nincompoops or our own nervous relatives—convince us to look backward through the rosy, sanitized lens of nostalgia. We mustn't live in fear that happiness will elude us if we don't follow a traditional script or play by *The Rules*.

A few years ago, Barbara Walters had a TV special celebrating—surprise—her TV specials. She did a retrospective of all the big stars she'd interviewed. Sucker that I am for insipid celebrity gossip, I watched the whole thing.

And watching it, I learned something about happiness from Eddie Murphy, of all people.

Walters showed two interviews with him. In the first, Murphy was newly famous; he'd just moved into a mansion and was extremely awkward and defensive.

In the second interview, conducted five years later, he seemed ebullient and joked easily with Walters. "So, Eddie, are you happy now?" she asked him.

Eddie smiled thoughtfully. Sometimes he is and sometimes he isn't, he answered plainly. And I'm paraphrasing a little, but he said, essentially, "Barbara, I used to think that happiness was something you achieved. But now I realize that it's not. It's just something that comes and goes, and comes and goes again, no matter who you are or what you're doing."

This sounds, like, Du-uh. But actually, it's not something we hear very often in our culture these days. Usually, we're constantly being told that there is something terribly and fundamentally wrong with us if we don't look like Cameron Diaz. Or that happiness is a commodity: We'll achieve it if we just buy enough cool stuff. Or we're prescribed "happy pills" like Zoloft. Talk about chemical warfare.

In writing this book, it's been my intention to offer women inspiration, wit, and tools for "intelligent resistance" to all such whacked-out messages. And yet, in doing so, I think it's important to emphasize that there are no easy or foolproof answers. Kierkegaard once said that "anxiety is the dizziness of freedom." Well, with our new freedom, we gals are going to experience both dizziness and anxiety. So be it. We might as well find some way we can enjoy the hell out of it, if we can.

Besides, five hundred years ago most women were peasants or slaves and had the status of chattel. A hundred years ago, women couldn't vote, own property, or wear pants. Forty years ago, women could be discriminated against in the workforce and raped by their husbands without recourse. Thirty years ago, we couldn't get legal abortions and got fired for being pregnant.

In comparison, I'd say we chicks today have it pretty easy.

We're in the best position ever to conquer the world, to flourish and prevail. We have the guts, the tools, the vision. We have the brains and the attitude. Some of us even have the clothes. So why look backward or give in to our fears? As my grandma used to say, "The world will be more heartbreaking than you know, and more beautiful than you'll ever imagine."

So let's follow our own path, stand tall, and don't take any shit. And while we're at it, have a good laugh.

Acknowledgments

Many people helped shape and inspire this book, yet several were so instrumental I have to single them out for praise, public embarrassment, and my undying gratitude. In a proverbial champagne toast, I raise my glass to the following:

First and foremost, to the Power Babes: my agent, Irene Skolnick, and my editor at Warner Books, Amy Einhorn, for having immediate faith in this project and taking me on in all my hypercaffeinated glory. Kudos, too, to editorial assistants Sandra Bark and Shannon Beatty.

To my Research Goddess, Allison Kuttner. Without her resourcefulness, I probably would have just made stuff up to suit my purposes, thereby becoming the epitome of the very same stupid and expedient culture I just spent two hundred–plus pages critiquing. Thank you, Allison, for keeping me honest.

To the Nominees for Sainthood: Desa Sealy Ruffin and Bari Handelman actually read through rough drafts of this repeatedly, indulging me to a degree some might consider criminally negligent. Ditto for Stefanie Weiss, who listened to me talk about this book ad nauseam, yet still managed to offer terrific editorial advice. Ditto for Sarah Ferguson (not the duchess), who literally gave me a hallowed Room of One's Own.

To my Sister-in-Arms, Ophira Edut, who continually serves as inspiration and editrix.

To the Pink Posse, a generous inner circle of smartass females who regularly laughed with me and let me turn their private lives into object lessons. Major props go to, in alphabetical order: Melinda Anderson, Karen Archia, Laurie Mintzer Edberg, Candy Fletcher, Robin Gellman, Carolyn Hunt, Sara Pines, Hannah Serota-Campbell, Amy Simon, Jennifer Sosin, Cecilie Surasky, and Suzanna Zwerling.

To the Good Guys: Mark Torok and Christopher Campbell, for their unwitting contributions.

To my Supportive Cohorts: Eddy Gattis, Ann Kurzius, Kate Mattos, Connie Morris, David Sheridan, and Jim Whitmire, who helped me clear my decks and carve out the time to write.

To the Great Dane, Pernille Chambliss, who kept me sane while I did this.

To my Fearless Family: Goddess bless (and help) my parents, David and Ellen, who never dissuaded me from speaking my mind and who had the foresight to give me my brother, John Seeger Gilman, who has humored and supported me like no one else.

That is, except for the last-but-not-least person on my list: my strong and stunning partner, Bob Stefanski, who makes everything in this world seem more entertaining and possible. Thank you, Bob, for your love, patience, and endorsement.

ALSO AVAILABLE FROM WARNER BOOKS

IN THESE GIRLS, HOPE IS A MUSCLE
A True Story of Hoop Dreams and One Very Special Team
by Madeleine Blais

They were a talented team with a near-perfect record. But for five straight years, when it came to the crunch of the playoffs, the Amherst Lady Hurricanes somehow lacked the scrappy desire to go all the way. Now finally, it is their season to test their passion for the sport and their loyalty to each other. This is the fierce, funny, and intimate look into the minds and hearts of one group of girls and their quest for success and, most important of all, respect.

"Beautifully written . . . a celebration of girls and athletics."
—*USA Today*

❧

LITTLE GIRLS IN PRETTY BOXES
The Making and Breaking of Elite Gymnasts and Figure Skaters
by Joan Ryan

This book chronicles the real world of women's gymnastics and figure skating that happens away from the cameras, at the training camps and in the private lives of these teenage competitors. From starvation diets and debilitating injuries to the brutal tactics of trainers, it portrays the horrors endured by girls at the hands of their coaches and sometimes their own families. An acclaimed exposé that has already helped reform the Olympics, it's now updated to reflect the latest developments in these sports.

"Scathing . . . profoundly important."
—*San Francisco Chronicle*

more . . .

GIRL POWER

Personal Writings from Teenage Girls
by Hillary Carlip

In this extraordinary book, discover the secrets and deepest needs of girls from across the country—the thoughts, the fears, and the dreams of girls between the ages of thirteen and nineteen. Hear from teen mothers and beauty queens, girl rappers and farm girls, surfers and sorority sisters. Theirs are voices that are too often silenced or ignored, and in this stunning collection, they dare to reveal things that will enlighten and touch readers.

"Moving, striking, and important . . . a beacon in the darkness. Should be required reading for all young women."
—**Melissa Etheridge**

❧

About the Author

SUSAN JANE GILMAN has written commentary for the *New York Times, Ms., US,* and the *Los Angeles Times,* among others. Winner of several literary awards for her fiction and essays, she is a native New Yorker who has recently lived in Washington, D.C. and Geneva, Switzerland.